Reading Strategies

for the
Social Studies Classroom

Dr. Judith Irvin

HOLT, RINEHART AND WINSTON

A Harcourt Classroom Education Company

Austin · New York · Orlando · Atlanta · San Francisco · Boston · Dallas · Toronto · London

Cover: (foreground), Victoria Smith/HRW Photo; (background composite), Tim Bierber/ The Image Bank and Yellow Dog Productions/The Image Bank.

Printed in the United States of America
ISBN 0-03-065354-1

4 5 6 7 8 9   095   04 03 02

Table of Contents

Introduction

by Dr. Judith Irvin

By all accounts, I was a pretty good social studies teacher. During my many years of middle and high school teaching, I worked primarily with students who struggled with reading and writing. In my desperate attempt to help students learn the content of history, geography, world cultures, economics and so forth, I did what many good teachers did—I avoided the textbook. I engaged the students in inquiry, conducted simulations, showed videos, presented documents, created maps and charts, and led lively discussions and debates. Oh, I trotted the textbook out occasionally to use the pictures, diagrams, and primary source material, but it was simply too difficult (or too much trouble) to ask students to read it.

When I did ask students to read, I used the only approach I knew—round-robin reading. This familiar classroom practice of having different students read paragraphs and stopping periodically to discuss the major points or key vocabulary worked about as well as it did when I was in school. I noticed that the students began the session by counting the paragraphs to see which one would be assigned to them and scanning them for difficult words and length, just like I did when I was in school. No one really concentrated on what was being read. Rather, they agonized until their turn was over. The strong readers were bored, and the struggling readers were embarrassed. I modified this approach by having students volunteer or call on the next reader. In middle school I often alternated between boys and girls. I even employed what is now called jump-in-reading, in which volunteers just start reading when another stops. These modifications created slightly more interest in the material at hand, but I would not say they stimulated any thought or motivation to learn. So, in desperation, I simply gave up using the textbooks and placed them neatly on the shelves.

In retrospect, I taught students about their world, their government, their social system, and themselves. After all, that is why I was receiving a salary. But I did not help them become more proficient readers and writers, and, unfortunately, lack of these skills would make it more difficult for them to learn in the future. If I could only go back knowing what I know now.

My motivation for writing *Reading Strategies for the Social Studies Classroom* is to assist you, the social studies teacher, in implementing learning strategies that not only help students read and write more proficiently but engage them in learning the content that is so important to their understanding of themselves and their world. This project is, perhaps, one way I can give something back to the profession I care so much about—teaching social studies.

How I Learned to Teach Reading

Shortly after I decided to shelve my textbooks, our principal made the announcement, "Every teacher is a teacher of reading." Really? I had a master's degree in social studies education. I took courses in values education, inquiry, and concept development. What did I know about teaching reading? Being a good team player, I asked how I was supposed to accomplish this feat. I learned that I was supposed to set aside my beloved history and important geography to teach "finding the main idea," "determining details," and "locating information" through skills worksheets provided to me by the reading specialist. Trying this approach in my class generated even less enthusiasm than round-robin reading.

I became very resentful. I nodded dutifully at in-service sessions and talked about how important it was that students read and write better. I perused the standardized tests and agreed to incorporate skills sessions into my teaching. I participated in lengthy discussions in my department. Then I shut my door and went back to my way of teaching social studies because I was annoyed at being asked not to teach what was vitally important to me and to my students. The next year I was quite relieved when my school administrators decided that some other educational issue was more important than teaching reading.

After a few more years, I began my Ph.D. work in social studies education at Indiana University. During this time, I began taking courses in reading education. I learned about whole language (thematic instruction), pre-reading instruction (inquiry), and vocabulary development (concept development). To my amazement, I discovered that I had been using very effective learning strategies through the methods I had applied in my classroom. But I fell short of helping students apply those concepts when reading their textbooks.

I finished my doctorate in reading education and wrote a dissertation that incorporated both social studies theory and reading theory. In all fairness to my former principal, the field of reading education was redefined during the period between his mandate and my doctoral studies. The field of adolescent literacy has continued to evolve over the past two decades. These ideas are supported by new research and theories that hold many practical classroom applications.

The Study of Reading

The research in reading falls into four categories: the text, the context of learning, the learner, and learning strategies. These four factors can be conveniently separated for the purposes of discussion, but of course they are intricately linked and occur simultaneously. Figure 1 shows how these influencing factors may interact with each other.

Figure 1

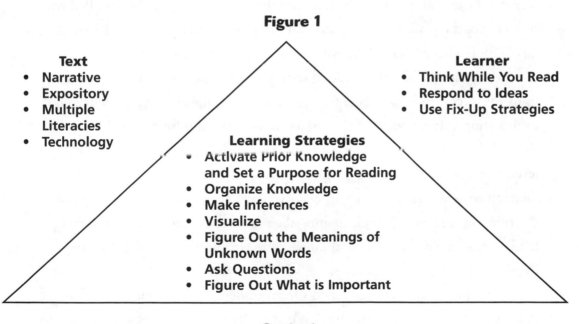

Text
- Narrative
- Expository
- Multiple Literacies
- Technology

Learner
- Think While You Read
- Respond to Ideas
- Use Fix-Up Strategies

Learning Strategies
- Activate Prior Knowledge and Set a Purpose for Reading
- Organize Knowledge
- Make Inferences
- Visualize
- Figure Out the Meanings of Unknown Words
- Ask Questions
- Figure Out What is Important

Context
- Developmental Tasks
- School Culture

Triangle diagram adapted from *Strategic Learning in the Content Areas*, edited by D. Cook, 1989. Reprinted by permission of **Wisconsin Department of Public Instruction**.

The Text. Good readers have expectations from text, depending on the way it looks or their purpose for reading. When you jump into the bathtub at night with a romance novel, you rarely take a highlighter with you. Your purpose for reading is not to understand or remember something, but simply to enjoy the story. Being residents of Florida, after a hurricane my husband and I read our homeowners' insurance policy very, very carefully. We may stop and ponder over words such as *contingent upon* and discuss the possible interpretation of these words. This is not the same way I read poetry or a menu. Good readers are flexible across a variety of text and know how to adjust their reading, depending on their purpose; poor readers read everything pretty much the same way.

During the elementary years, children read primarily narrative text. Whether they read in a basal series or library books, children are pretty good at knowing how a story goes. Likewise, teachers naturally offer instruction in how to read a story by thinking about the setting or characters or by answering comprehension questions. Yet when elementary teachers embark on a social studies lesson, they generally jump straight to the content. They spend no time at all on *how* to read the textbook. When students enter middle school, the demands on reading informational or expository text are much greater, and often no one seems to be available to help them master this type of text. Textbooks filled with new concepts replace stories. Charts and diagrams replace pictures. The vocabulary is more difficult and often essential in understanding the text.

My analysis of the standardized testing programs created by many states leads me to conclude that these tests place a heavy emphasis on expository or informational items. Some of these tests are 60 percent informational items at the eighth-grade level and 80 percent informational items at the tenth-grade level. In addition, the writing portion of these very important tests require students to write informational or expository essays. In a sense, we have changed the rules on students by implementing these state tests that demand a higher level of thinking and analysis and much more flexibility in reading than are involved in simple narrative texts.

Who in middle and high schools helps students become more successful at reading and writing expository text? When I ask this question of a school faculty, the English/language arts teachers point to the social studies and science teachers because they are the ones with these types of textbooks. The social studies and science teachers point to English/language arts teachers because they "do" words. Even when students attend a reading class, what is usually taught is more narrative and on a lower reading level. What happens when that same student enters your social studies class and no one has helped him or her to really understand how to read the textbook?

Teachers often comment that students do not read anything outside of school. In reality, they read all kinds of text. They read e-mail, notes from friends, magazines, TV listings, cereal boxes, instructions for video games, T-shirts, movie posters, signs, song lyrics, and so much more. When we say that adolescents do not read, we mean they do not read "our" stuff. The truth is that students may read, but if they are not good at reading narrative and expository text, they cannot be successful at school.

This notion of acknowledging and respecting the literacy of adolescents outside of school is called multiple literacies. Simply, we can connect to our students' "real world" literacy by creating links to what we want them to read in school. When students read song lyrics, we can make connections to poetry. When students see movies, we can make connections to short stories. When students peruse Internet sites about rock stars, we can make connections to biographies. When students read instructions to video games, we can make connections to expository text. It is tempting for teachers to hide from the "real world" amidst textbooks and curriculum guides. But unless we recognize and provide links to the kinds of reading and writing that adolescents encounter in the "real world," they may never value what we are trying to teach them.

In addition, technology will continue to change the way we think about literacy and the demands of being literate in our society. When students go to the Internet for information, they must realize that anything, literally anything—from fact to opinion to advertisements to propaganda—can be posted on the World Wide Web. Students must be taught to become critical readers, listeners, and viewers in our world of ever exploding information.

Assignments must change as well. When my son was in ninth grade, I observed him "writing a report." He inserted the encyclopedia CD into our computer, located the appropriate information, dumped it to disk, double spaced it, and proceeded to remove anything that looked like an encyclopedia entry, such as pronunciation guides. As I walked through the room and read the screen from over his shoulder, I asked him what *dilapidated* meant. He told me but added, "Well, you are right, my teacher probably wouldn't think I know that word," and he substituted the word *poor*. So, he continued his report writing by substituting less sophisticated synonyms for difficult words. He printed the report and handed it in the next day never having read the material, let alone writing it. He got an A.

Well, we had a long discussion about plagiarism. But the incident caused me to think how technology has changed, or should change, the work we assign. Brandon would have to think if he had to display that information in a concept map, synthesize it into a summary, or explain it to someone else. The strategies in this book are designed to accomplish these goals. They will engage students in learning material, provide the vehicle for them to organize and reorganize concepts, and extend their understanding through writing.

The Context for Learning. Middle and high school students are immersed in life. The developmental tasks of becoming autonomous, forming a positive self concept, learning social skills, progressing academically, and engaging in abstract thinking are all very important life work. While it is easy for adults to focus on the defiance or egocentrism of these developmental tasks (autonomy or abstract thinking), the sometimes annoying behavior of many adolescents is a necessary stepping-stone to becoming an adult. It is essential that teachers accommodate these developmental tasks. Through social studies content, we can assist students in moving successfully toward adulthood with a better understanding of their world and themselves.

To facilitate the developmental tasks of adolescence, you, as educators, can also create positive climates in schools and classrooms that reward effort as well as ability, provide a relevant curriculum, and motivate students to learn. I believe that we, as teachers, have to dig deep and ask ourselves, "What is worth knowing for adolescents in today's society?" and "How do we present this knowledge?" so that it makes sense to the lives and experiences of our students. My friend and colleague, Doug Buehl, who is a reading-resource teacher in Madison, Wisconsin, asks, "If you met one of your students in the grocery store five years from now, what would you expect for that person to remember? That is, what is the content you would be really disturbed if the student didn't remember in five years?"[1] If we present that material in a way that connects to the lives of students, I believe they will remember it and, perhaps, even use that information to learn more.

The Learner. Our students come to us knowing a lot of stuff. This "stuff," or prior knowledge, may or may not be useful in school. All of us have extensive prior knowledge about our lives, our world, and our families. This prior knowledge is made up of all that we have experienced, including our values, beliefs, and culture. You can think of this accumulated prior knowledge like a file cabinet. We all have multiple file folders, skinny or thick, on a variety of topics. For example, I have a big thick file folder on soccer. My husband is a soccer coach; my daughter plays soccer in college; my son played soccer; and I played on a recreational women's team. I can illustrate the function of a sweeper or a striker and explain an off-sides trap. I have enthusiastically watched hundreds of hours of soccer. On the other hand, I have a skinny file folder on football. Although I teach in a university where football reigns supreme, I rarely attend a game and do not know very much about the game or the players.

Sometimes our job as teachers is to hand students a file folder and have them label it and put some things in it (building background information). Sometimes our job is to have students retrieve those file folders and read through them (activating prior knowledge). Students often need help retrieving information because even if they know something about a topic, they do not tend to use that information unless it is activated. Finally, sometimes our job is to help students organize their file folders or the information within their file folders, placing labels on different parts so they can use this information in a new context (organizing knowledge). Selecting an appropriate strategy often depends on how much prior knowledge students possess about the topic at hand. A good guiding principle is that students cannot learn anything new unless they are able to connect it to something they already know. Figure 2 shows how the components of comprehension work together as readers try to make sense of text.

[1] Quote by **Doug Buehl**. Reprinted by permission of the author.

Figure 2

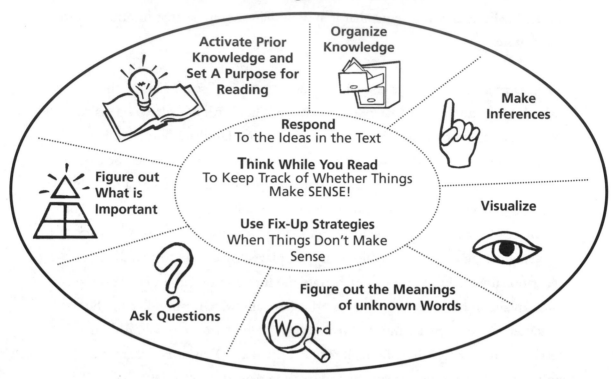

Adapted oval diagram from Margaret Boling Mullin, Wydown Middle School, 6500 Wydown Blvd., Clayton, MO 63105. Reprinted by permission of **Margaret Boling Mullin**.

Think While You Read. Many students see reading, especially a social studies text, as something to "get through," rather than something to absorb, integrate, synthesize, and extend. So they may put in the time, and their eyes may glance over the words, but they do not learn or remember the information because they have not thought about it.

Respond to the Ideas in the Text. When students are engaged in the reading the text, they respond to the ideas in some way. They ask themselves questions; they organize the ideas in a map, and/or they connect the ideas with what they already know.

Use Fix-Up Strategies. Strong readers keep track of whether or not things make sense to them and do something to "fix up" their comprehension if things do not make sense. They might use the glossary, reread, read ahead, think about the topic, or ask someone.

Learning Strategies. As you read through the strategies in this book, you will encounter the icons shown on Figure 2. These icons are to help you recognize how the strategy fits into the larger context of comprehension.

Activate Prior Knowledge and Set a Purpose for Reading. Before reading, good readers activate what they know about a topic by looking at the table of contents, glossary, titles, captions, section headings, and/or graphics. They pause and make connections from the text to their experience and prior knowledge. They may skim the structure of the text for main ideas and think about what they will be expected to do with the reading, such as take a test, write a report, explain a concept to someone, or apply the information in a different setting.

Organize Knowledge. During and after reading, strong readers summarize the major ideas and state them in their own words. They may skim the text and reread portions to create a concept map, write a summary, create an outline, or take notes. It is the organization and reorganization of knowledge that helps students understand, remember, and use the major concepts presented in the text.

Make Inferences. Good readers connect what is in their head (prior knowledge) with what is on the page. For example, if they see a building with an onion-shaped dome, they might accurately infer that the setting was in Russia. Strong readers make numerous inferences throughout their reading. Accurate inference making depends on the background knowledge of the reader.

Visualize. Students today are bombarded with visual information, whether through video games, television, or the Internet. They must analyze and interpret visual information they receive. Proficient readers can visualize the information presented in text. Non-proficient readers, on the other hand, do not seem to be able to use their imagination to create pictures in their minds. Having students sketch, create concept maps, diagrams, charts, or other visual representations of the information assists students in creating these visual images.

Figure Out the Meanings of Unknown Words. As students read increasingly complex text, they naturally encounter words they do not know. Previewing text for key vocabulary and using context and structural analysis can help students increase their vocabularies and comprehend the text. The use of context, syntax (the way that words function in a sentence), and structural analysis together are the most effective tools for figuring out the meanings of unknown words.

Ask Questions. Before and during reading, strong readers ask themselves questions such as, "What do I know about this topic?", "Why did the pioneers settle where they did?", or "What is the meaning of a concept in bold print?"

These questions indicate that students are thinking about the reading and connecting the ideas in the text to their prior knowledge.

Figure out What Is Important. One of the most common question types on any standardized test is "finding the main idea." To comprehend text, readers must identify, remember, and summarize the major ideas presented in the text. Figuring out what is important in the text should be tied to the purpose for reading. Taking notes from text, constructing a concept map, or creating an outline all involve identifying what is important in the text.

Once you are comfortable with these basics of learning theory as presented in Figure 2, you can talk to students about how effective and efficient learning takes place. If talking about effective reading behaviors becomes a natural part of classroom instruction, students can add these ideas to their repertoire and hopefully become stronger, more flexible, and more proficient readers.

Skills and Strategies

During a soccer game, players demonstrate a high level of skill, but they cannot win the game without strategy. Players generally do not think much about the basics of ball handling when they receive a pass—dribbling is automatic. In order to get the ball in the net, however, players need a strategy. They have to keep in mind how many minutes remain in the game, notice the placement of the goalie, and anticipate where their teammate will be to receive the cross.

Veteran teachers have heard the terms *skills* and *strategies* thrown around professional journals and meetings for many years. *Skills* are automatic, fairly low thinking, and consistent in application. Skills take practice. This fact became abundantly clear to me the first time I was in the car with my sixteen-year-old son and his brand new driver's license. Making a left-hand turn in traffic takes a high level of driving skill and, initially, a lot of concentration. Checking both mirrors, timing the change of the light, gauging the distances of oncoming cars, and signaling the turn became automatic behaviors for him after practice. He can now negotiate the same turn in traffic while carrying on a conversation and eating a candy bar.

While driving gets easier and more habitual with practice and we perform this function automatically, we all need a plan when charting unfamiliar territory. We consult a map, ask someone for directions, and formulate a strategy for getting to our destination. A *strategy* is an overall plan requiring higher levels of reasoning. It is flexible in application and involves awareness and reflection.

Proficient reading takes both the execution of skills and a strategy for fulfilling the intended purpose for reading. Taking notes from a textbook, after practice, becomes a fairly automatic process of identifying the most important points and recording them in a way that can be used later. But it takes a strategy to put the parts and pieces together to write a report. Strong readers have a strategy *before* they read to connect what they know about the topic (setting, theme, issue) of the text, and they remember their purpose. They continue their strategy *during* reading to maintain concentration and reflect on the ideas in the text and *after* reading to organize major points to fulfill the purpose for reading. The learning strategies you will explore in this book are designed to engage students in the behaviors of strong reading until these behaviors become part of their repertoire. Strategies are associated with a newer view of the reading process. It is tempting to think that strategies must replace skills, but both are important components of successful reading.

Helping Struggling Readers Become Strong Readers

Struggling readers can do the same thing as strong readers, but they need more help, more support, and more scaffolding to perform in this way. For example, my husband recently purchased a new boat. One of the things that makes this boat desirable is that it sits very high in the water, which is wonderful when you are in the boat looking down. On the first day of scalloping season, my daughter and I jumped into the water and began snorkeling for the illusive scallop. Then it came time to get back in the boat. The platform and the one step were too high for me to reach. I wanted two more steps to be able to approach the platform—the scaffolding I needed to begin the task of climbing back in the boat. Struggling readers have a similar dilemma. They often have difficulty getting started with a task, and then they easily give up.

To avoid this problem as you try out each strategy, make sure you first introduce the strategy with fairly simple reading so that students learn the steps of the strategy and do not have to face the additional challenge of difficult text. As you select an appropriate strategy, consider the prior knowledge that students have about the topic under study, the type of text being used, and the purpose for the reading. You will find that some strategies lend themselves better to the study of world cultures, and others are more applicable to the study of history or economics. You will also find that you prefer some strategies over others. My purpose is to provide you with options to use in any teaching and learning context. It is my fervent hope that you find that these strategies enhance your social studies instruction by engaging students more actively in learning.

Good Luck and Best Wishes,

Dr. Judith Irvin

Read More about It

Irvin, J. L. 1998. *Reading and the middle school student: Strategies to enhance literacy* (2nd edition). Boston: Allyn and Bacon.

Irvin, J. L., Buehl, D., and Klemp, R. 2002. *Reading and the high school student: Strategies to enhance literacy.* Boston: Allyn and Bacon.

Irvin, J. L., Lunstrum, J. P., Lynch-Brown, C., and Shepard, M. F. 1995. *Enhancing social studies instruction through reading and writing strategies.* Washington, D. C.: National Council for the Social Studies.

Strategy 1

Previewing Text

When facing a textbook reading assignment, most students just plow in and try to finish it as quickly as possible. They may leaf through the chapter or passage to see how long it is, noticing how many pages they can skip because of pictures or graphs. Proficient readers, on the other hand, take a moment to consider the following things *before* they begin a textbook reading assignment:

Purpose of the reading

Important ideas

Connection to prior knowledge

This strategy of previewing text is therefore known as PIC. You can use the PIC strategy to help your students develop good reading habits by encouraging them to spend just a few moments organizing their thinking and setting their goals before beginning a reading assignment. In addition, students think about the main idea of the passage before they start reading. After reading, they may change what they thought the main idea was or confirm that their prediction was correct.

How Can the Strategy Help My Students?

The PIC strategy can get your students into the all-important habits of setting a purpose for their reading, identifying the most important ideas, and connecting with what they already know. Often when students read, they do not think about what is really important to remember. Previewing reading assignments helps students focus on the most important information and facilitates storing that information in long-term memory. If students take a few moments to go through the steps described below, they will be more successful when they read—better understanding and remembering the text.

Getting Started

Step 1: *Purpose for Reading.* Make sure students know what to do with the information after reading (i.e., What is the assignment or purpose for reading? What will they do with the information?). Have them peruse the structure of the assignment, noting special features such as summaries or guiding questions. Ask students to use the table of contents, glossary, and index of the book to locate information.

Step 2: *Important Ideas.* Students should flip through the assignment, noting the headings that indicate the major points in the reading. They should try to understand how this passage fits within the larger chapter or unit. Students should also read the key vocabulary in boldfaced type or italics to see if those concepts are familiar to them. These are probably the most important ideas in the text.

Step 3: *Connect to What You Know.* Students need to think about what they know about the topic before starting to read. Encourage them to wonder about the topic, asking themselves, "What would I like to find out?" Finally, students should identify questions they want answered about the topic. They can use a chart like this one to organize their ideas.

What I Know about the Topic	What I Wonder about the Topic	Questions I Would Like to Have Answered

The Strategy in Action

The following steps show you how to implement the strategy. This activity is focused on the topic of society during Europe's Middle Ages.

Society in the Middle Ages

Even before the Vikings began their attacks, other invaders struck the Roman Empire, which included much of Europe and parts of Africa, Asia Minor, and the Middle East. These invaders included Germanic, Slav, and Hun raiders. In the late A.D. 400s, after continued invasions and economic and political troubles, the empire collapsed. This marked the beginning of Europe's **Middle Ages,** which continued until around A.D. 1350.

During the early Middle Ages, trade and communication networks broke down, city populations declined, and much of Europe experienced political disorder. During these difficult times, **feudalism**—a system of government in which people pledged loyalty to a lord in exchange for protection—gradually developed.

Nobles. Lords defended their **manors,** or large estates, with the help of people known as vassals. Vassals pledged to defend the lord and his property "against all malefactors [criminals] and invaders." Some of these vassals were warriors called knights.

Lords lived in large wooden or stone manor houses or castles, sometimes built with moats and high walls for defense. These noblemen fought in battles and managed their farmland, while noblewomen maintained the home and raised children.

Peasants. Peasants farmed the manor's land. Some peasants were tenants, who rented land from lords. Tenants could leave the manor at the end of their contracts. Other peasants were serfs, who lived on a particular manor's land for life in return for the protection of the lord. A number of peasants were slaves, who mostly worked as field laborers or servants. By the A.D. 1000s most slaves in western Europe had been freed. Most eventually became serfs.

Peasants worked hard and lived simple lives. Their houses usually had two rooms, one in which the family slept and ate and another for farm animals. Men spent most of their time plowing fields, planting seeds, and harvesting crops. Women and children weeded fields, tended farm animals, baked and cooked, and planted and harvested fruit trees and vegetable gardens. From an early age, children worked alongside their parents.

The Church. On manors the Catholic Church was the center of religious and social life. Both nobles and peasants attended mass with the local priest. Priests also cared for the sick and poor, counseled the rich and taught the young. Over time, the Catholic Church grew in wealth, land, and power throughout Europe. Church bishops often had a great deal of political influence through their roles as advisers to monarchs on spiritual matters.

Step 1: *Purpose for Reading.* Students would ask the following questions:
- What am I going to do with this information when I finish reading?
  My teacher said we were going to write a short paper comparing life in the Middle Ages and life today. We must include this information in a Venn diagram that compares and contrasts society in America today and society during the Middle Ages.
- How does this text fit in with the material before or after it?
  This section is within a chapter called Europe during the Middle Ages. This information on Society in the Middle Ages contains information on how people lived. Later, it looks like I'll find out about how some of the nations of Europe developed and some of the inventions people came up with.

Step 2: *Important Ideas.* Students would ask the following questions:
- Is there anything in the table of contents, index, or glossary that can help me understand the "big ideas"?
  The words that are in boldfaced type are: Middle Ages, feudalism, *and* manors. *I know* Middle Ages *and* manor *but probably need to look more closely at* feudalism. *It is defined in the text, which matches the definition in the glossary.*

Glossary

feudalism System of government that arose during the Middle Ages, in which people are loyal to a lord in exchange for protection.

- What is the main idea of this text?

  Topic = Middle Ages

  Main Idea = Middle Ages and the roles nobles, peasants, and the church played in their society.

  I haven't read it yet, but it appears that this text is going to compare the nobles to the peasants and tell me about the role that the church played in society during the Middle Ages.

- What are the key vocabulary terms I should understand?

  Middle Ages

  feudalism

  manors

Step 3: **Connect to What You Know.** Students would use the chart below to help them connect to what they already know about this topic.

What I Know about the Topic	Questions I Would Like to Have Answered
People were poor.	Were knights soldiers?
Knights wore armor.	How did one become a lord?
Kings ruled.	Did the knights really wear armor?
It was a long time ago.	Were the nobles mean to the
They lived in castles with moats	peasants?
around them.	Was everybody a Catholic back
A society is how people live and	then?
work together.	Why was the church influential?

Using the Strategy in Your Classroom

After students have read the text, they should go back to their PIC preview, see if their questions were answered, and check to make sure they understand the key vocabulary. Feel free to vary the strategy as students become accustomed to previewing their assignments. You may wish to move from answering each question to having students address just the purpose for reading, important information about the topic, and connecting-to-prior-knowledge questions in a quick discussion or pre-reading assignment.

You can also add an after-reading component by asking students to discuss the questions they wanted answered in small groups or as a class. They may have some questions that were not answered in the text. These questions can be the basis of further research or projects.

Extending the Strategy

The diagrams, charts, maps, and pictures in a social studies book are included to help the reader understand the content. As students become more familiar with previewing, you may wish to direct their attention to the graphic features in the text, asking them in what ways these items will extend or support their learning.

The PIC strategy is simply a guide to help students preview the text before reading and focus on the most important points. It can be used in conjunction with other assignments or modified to serve as a basis for study for a test or writing a report. For example, you can ask students to sketch out a concept map or graphic organizer (see Strategies 3 and 4) before they read and to fill it in after they read. They can then use this organizer as a writing or study guide.

Some Final Thoughts

The purpose for previewing text is to get students to recognize the text's main idea. However, helping students identify the main idea of a text passage is often a difficult challenge. The main idea could be a theme, something important to students, or the first sentence in a paragraph. David Moore (1986) suggested that you engage students in stating what the text is about in one or two words (in this case, Middle Ages) and then add two or three other words to go with it (and the roles nobles, peasants, and the church played in society). This usually comes closer to the author's intended main idea.

When students first use PIC, the process will seem very time-consuming. But as they become more familiar with the format and steps, they will move through the strategy more quickly. Feel free to modify the strategy to suit the needs of your students.

Practice the Strategy

Use these online materials to guide your students as they practice the Previewing Text strategy.

internet **connect**

Online Resources
keyword: ST2Strategies

go.
hrw
.com

Read More about It

Chen, H. S. and Graves, M. F. 1998. Previewing challenging reading selections for ESL students. *Journal of Adolescent and Adult Literacy* 41 (7): 570–71.

Cunningham, J. W., and Moore, D. W. 1986. The confused world of main idea. In *Teaching main idea comprehension,* edited by J. Baumann. Newark, DE: International Reading Association.

Dana, C. 1989. Strategy families for disabled readers. *Journal of Reading* 33 (5): 30–35.

Huffman, L. E. 1996. What's in it for you? A student-directed text preview. *Journal of Adolescent and Adult Literacy* 40 (1): 56–57.

Salemblier, G. B. 1999. SCAN and RUN: A reading comprehension strategy that works. *Journal of Adolescent and Adult Literacy* 42 (5): 386–94.

Strategy 2
Understanding Text

When you come home at the end of the day and flip through the mail, you probably read the various items you have received quite differently. You expect to read a letter from a friend in a different way than you would read a notice from a lawyer you do not know. The items *look* different, use different vocabularies, and have different structures. You certainly read a catalog differently from the way you read song lyrics or poetry. Part of what strong readers know is how to adjust their reading, depending on the text and their purpose for reading that text.

A social studies textbook contains different forms of text. Students must interpret pictures, diagrams, figures, and charts. They read narrative accounts, diaries, and documents that support the major concepts. Then there is the text itself. Expository or informational text, such as a social studies book, is generally structured in one of five forms: (1) cause and effect, (2) compare and contrast, (3) description, (4) problem and solution, and (5) sequence or chronological order. Particular content lends itself more or less to one structure or another. For example, while history is generally conveyed in a sequence or chronological order, geography may be best learned in a descriptive format, and economics may lend itself to a cause-and-effect structure. In addition, one or more forms may be contained within a passage. The more that students can detect the structure of text, the better they can prepare themselves to think in a way that is consistent with that structure.

Signal or transition words usually indicate the structure of the text. Proficient readers intuitively notice the words that indicate what type of thinking is required while reading. Signal words tell readers what is coming up. When you see *for example* or *for instance,* you know that examples will follow. When you see the word *consequently,* you know that you will read about the effect to the cause you were reading about. Below is a chart with some of the most common signal or transition words.

Cause and Effect	Compare and Contrast	Description	Problem and Solution	Sequence or Chronological Order

because
since
consequently
this led to . . .
  so
if . . . then
nevertheless
accordingly
because of
as a result of
in order to
may be due to
for this reason
not only . . .
  but
	different from
	same as
	similar to
	as opposed to
	instead of
	although
	however
	compared with
	as well as
	either . . . or
	but
	on the other
	  hand
	unless
		for instance
		for example
		such as
		to illustrate
		in addition
		most
		  importantly
		another
		furthermore
		first,
		  second . . .
			Problem
			the question is
			a solution
			one answer is
				not long after
				next
				then
				initially
				before
				after
				finally
				preceding
				following
				on (date)
				over the years
				today
				when

An important reading strategy based on these words is called Double S: *S*ignal Words That Indicate *S*tructure. This strategy is designed to help students recognize and use signal words to detect the structure of text.

How Can the Strategy Help My Students?

Good readers are flexible thinkers. Signal or transition words such as *different from, same as,* or *compared with* indicate that the authors are presenting information will compare and contrast at least two ideas. This compare and contrast structure is read differently from one in which ideas are presented in a sequence or chronological order. Signal or transition words indicate what the structure of text might be. When students notice these words in the text, especially before reading, they tend to "get ready" to think in a certain way. Struggling readers need to have these words pointed out to them and to be instructed on the function of these words while reading or writing. In time, they should be able to use signal words and move to more complex forms of text.

When students are learning to write expository text and must demonstrate that skill on a task such as producing a sample for a standardized test, use of these signal or transition words helps them express their points more clearly. As students recognize and use transition words and the different structures of text, they will (1) comprehend text more effectively, (2) produce more coherent expository writing, and (3) think more clearly and flexibly.

Getting Started

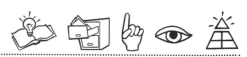

Step 1: Survey the Text. Have students flip through the text and list all the different types of reading they will have to perform, such as documents, charts, diagrams, or maps, a short story, or expository text. Usually, the expository text of a social studies textbook explains or informs the reader. But if primary source material, such as a diary, is presented, this may be read differently. The primary source probably supports one or more of the major points presented in the text.

Step 2: Identify the Signal Words. Using a blank transparency, have students circle transition words in the text. Some students prefer to highlight photocopied pages of text or attach "sticky" notes to help them locate the transition words. Alternatively, they may simply generate a list. Whatever the vehicle, students need to identify the signal words present in the text.

Step 3: Identify the Structure of the Text. Individually or in small groups, students should discuss what they think the main structure of the text may be (cause and effect, compare and contrast, description, problem and solution, and sequence or chronological order). They would ask themselves: "What kind of thinking will be necessary to understand the information in the text?" and "How would I best display the information after reading?"

Step 4: Predict the Main Idea of the Passage. Using what they know about the signal words and the structure of the text, students would write a sentence stating what they think the main idea of this passage may be.

Step 5: Read the Text.

Step 6: **Revisit the Main Idea Prediction.** After reading, students should go back to their prediction of the main idea of the passage. They may then use a graphic organizer to display the information, write a summary, or in some other way organize what they have read.

The Strategy in Action

The following steps show you how to implement the strategy. This activity is centered around the topic of water usage in the American West in the 1800s and today.

Linking Past to Present:
Water Usage in the West

When the Mormons arrived at the Great Salt Lake in Utah on July 24, 1847, they saw a barren plain. The Mormons, however, considered the place their Promised Land. They quickly dammed one of the streams that came down from the mountains, flooded the soil, and planted their first crops. Within a few weeks, 1,800 more settlers had arrived.

Brigham Young's welcoming words to the new settlers expressed the Mormons' belief in cooperation to make the best use of their scarce resources:

> "[T] here shall be no private ownership of the streams that come out of the canyons, nor the timber that grows on the hills. These belong to the people, all the people."

Mormon leaders allowed farmers only enough water to properly irrigate their fields. This leadership and cooperation helped the Mormons build a thriving agricultural community in the Utah desert.

Over the years, as more and more settlers made their way west, the U.S. government helped them meet the demands of the harsh environment. In the 1860s agents from the Department of Agriculture taught farmers on the Great Plains how to dig deep to find water. The department also introduced farmers to planting and harvesting techniques that conserved valuable water resources.

Then in 1902 the government established the Bureau of Reclamation—part of the Department of the Interior—to construct irrigation works. These projects enabled farmers to settle and grow crops on even more western lands. Because water supplies were concentrated in a few areas in the West, the Bureau of Reclamation built dams, reservoirs, and canals to bring additional water to dry regions.

Today the bureau manages all the water in the 17 states west of the Mississippi River. It delivers water to about 10 million acres of land and provides flood control and community assistance during droughts. One of the agency's most important goals is to increase water availability to the millions of people who live in the West. To do so, it uses technology, expertise, and cooperation. In 1997 U.S. Secretary of the Interior Bruce Babbitt announced that water from the Colorado River would be transferred to cities in California, not just to farms. Babbitt was confident that the new plan would benefit everybody. "If we keep at it," he stated, "we will be able to assure that every need will be addressed."

The Theodore Roosevelt Dam on the Salt River in Arizona is one of many modern dams controlling water flows throughout the Southwest.

North Wind Picture Archive

Step 1: **Survey the Text.** Students looking at this passage should notice the following things:
- *The major heading Linking Past to Present indicates how some action in the past may have affected life for people today.*
- *The picture of the Theodore Roosevelt Dam*
- *The text within quotation marks indicates a speech or diary.*

Step 2: **Identify the Signal Words.** The following signal words can be found in this passage:
- *When*
- *On July 24, 1847*
- *Within a few weeks*
- *Over the years*
- *In the late 1800s*
- *Then in 1902*
- *Today*
- *In 1997*

Step 3: **Identify the Structure.** These signal words indicate a sequence or chronological order to the text. Students should discuss the possibilities and then discuss how they may best display or organize the information when they are finished reading. This decision, of course, depends on the purpose for the reading.

Step 4: **Predict the Main Idea of the Passage.** The students' main idea prediction should be similar to this one: *Decisions about how water was used during the westward movement still influence people's lives today.*

Step 5: **Read the Text.**

Step 6: **Revisit the Main Idea Prediction.** Yes, this passage was about how the Mormons protected water usage from the early days of their settlement and how people today benefit from those wise decisions. An excerpt from Brigham Young's welcoming speech emphasized this major point.

Using the Strategy in Your Classroom

We know that good readers use signal or transition words to help guide their understanding and their thinking. Struggling readers do not. So teachers can help struggling readers to recognize and use signal words through Double S.

This does not mean asking students to memorize lists of words. Some teachers find it effective to post signal words on posters around the room or give students a page to put in their notebooks. They should also add their own as they find them in the text. In time, they will use these words more intuitively, and they will not need to go through the steps of identifying signal words before reading.

Discussing the structure of text is a little more difficult. The best way for students to "see" the structure is through graphic organizers (presented in Strategies 3 and 4). The more that students have these conversations about text, the more proficient they will become at recognizing and using text structure to guide their thinking.

Extending the Strategy

After students practice locating signal words and identifying text structure, you can link this strategy with Strategy 3: Using Graphic Organizers or Strategy 4: Constructing Concept Maps. This strategy may also be linked to the PIC technique you learned in Strategy 1.

Traditionally, reading and writing have been taught separately. But this practice with Signal Words and Structure in the Double S strategy can help students write expository pieces more effectively as well. Writing expository text is a major component of most state assessments. Social studies teachers can either link the reading and writing practice themselves or work with the English/language arts teacher to help create these connections for students.

Some Final Thoughts

Unfortunately, not all texts are written in a format that has an identifiable. structure. Similarly, no signal words may be present in the text. The text may also change structure within the passage. These more complex structures demand increasingly sophisticated reading ability. However, the Double S strategy can begin students along that road to becoming independent learners.

Practice the Strategy

Use these online materials to guide your students as they practice the
Understanding Text strategy.

Read More about It

Britton, B. K., Woodward, A. and Binkley, M., Eds. 1993. *Learning from text-books: theory and practice.* Hillsdale, NJ: Lawrence Erlbaum Associates.

Garner, R. and Alexander, P. A. Eds. 1994. *Beliefs about text and instruction with text.* Hillsdale, NJ: Lawrence Erlbaum Associates.

Harvey, S. 1998. *Nonfiction matters.* York, ME: Stenhouse Publishers.

McMackin, M. C. 1998. Using narrative picture books to build awareness of expository text structure. *Reading Horizons* 39 (1): 7–20.

Quiocho, A. 1997. The quest to comprehend expository text: Applied classroom research. *Journal of Adolescent and Adult Literacy* 40 (6): 450–54.

Strategy 3
Using Graphic Organizers

Graphic organizers are made up of lines, arrows, boxes, and circles that show the relationships among ideas. They are sometimes called webs, semantic maps, graphic representations, or clusters. These graphic organizers have the potential to help students organize their thinking and their knowledge. While social studies textbooks contain many types of text, the largest portion is expository or informational. Expository text has five major structures: (1) cause and effect, (2) compare and contrast, (3) description, (4) problem and solution, and (5) sequence or chronological order. In this strategy, four types of text structure will be presented. Description will be presented in Strategy 4 because this type of text is best displayed with a concept map. The four types of text structure with accompanying graphic organizers are shown below.

Cause and Effect
Cause and effect patterns show the relationship between results and the ideas or events that made the results occur.

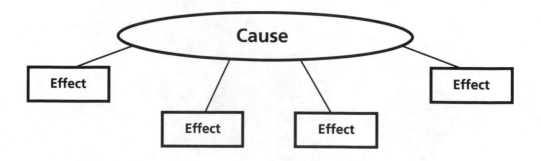

Problem and Solution

Problem-solution patterns identify at least one problem, offer one or more solutions to the problem, and explain or predict outcomes of the solutions.

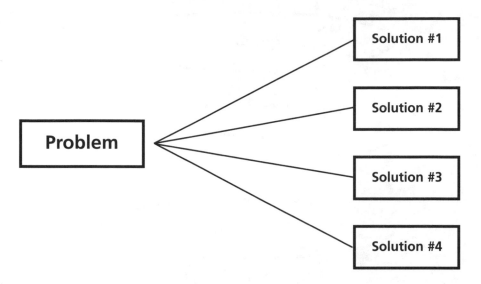

Compare and Contrast

Compare-and-contrast diagrams point out similarities and differences between two concepts or ideas.

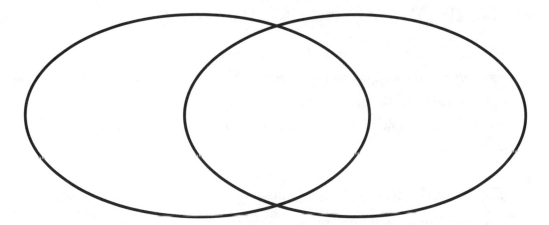

Sequence or Chronological Order

Sequence or chronological-order diagrams show events or ideas in the order in which they happened.

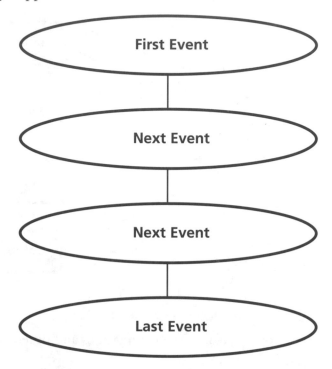

How Can the Strategy Help My Students?

The way that ideas are presented in a textbook dictates what type of thinking is necessary to understand and remember those ideas. Graphic organizers help students visualize the connections between and among ideas. They also help students organize knowledge so they can use it later to study for a test or write a report. The act of organizing information engages students in learning and helps them make connections to what they already know. In addition, discussing which graphic organizer might best display the information helps students "see" and use the structure of text to understand and remember more effectively.

Getting Started

Any single piece of text can be displayed in more than one way, depending on the purpose for reading and the reader's prior knowledge on the topic. Below are the basic steps in one approach to using graphic organizers.

Step 1: Students preview the material to be read.

Step 2: Students hypothesize which graphic organizer would be best to display the information and their understanding of the material.

Step 3: Students read the text silently, taking notes.

Step 4: Students work in cooperative groups to create a graphic representation of their understanding of the text.

Step 5: Students present the finished product to others in the class.

The Strategy in Action

The following steps show you how to implement the strategy. This activity is centered around the topic of printing money.

Step 1: Students preview the passage, Printing Money.

Step 2: Students hypothesize which of the four graphic organizers displayed earlier would be best to display the information and their understanding of the material. Their discussion should include the purpose for their reading, and hopefully, they should note any signal or transition words that may indicate the type of thinking required for the reading and the best way to display the information. Be sure to tell students that the organizers can be modified to meet their needs. For example, the cause-and-effect organizer has three effects, but the text may only state one or two.

Step 3: Students read the text silently, taking notes.

Printing Money

The U.S. Constitution states, "The Congress shall have Power . . . to coin Money." This passage gives the federal government alone the right to issue legal currency, or money, for the nation. However, until the mid-1800s, many state banks could print bank notes. These notes could be exchanged at the bank that issued them for their value in gold or silver coins.

As a result, there were many types of bank notes but little regulation of them. Banks often refused to accept or to honor the value of other banks' notes. The issuing of so many types of bank notes disrupted economic transaction. The federal government, therefore, stopped the states' issuing of bank notes and developed a national currency in the mid-1860s.

In the past 100 or so years, the government has made some changes to the money it issues. The U.S. Treasury discontinued printing the $500, $1,000, and $10,000 bills and introduced the $2 bill and the Susan B. Anthony dollar coin. The Treasury also has worked on redesigning paper money to make it harder to counterfeit. These new bills feature larger portraits than the older bills did. As *Time* magazine writes of the new $100 bill, Benjamin Franklin "now dominates the bill like a movie star in a newspaper advertisement."

Step 4: Students work in groups to create a graphic representation of their understanding of the text. Students may display their work as follows:

Cause and Effect

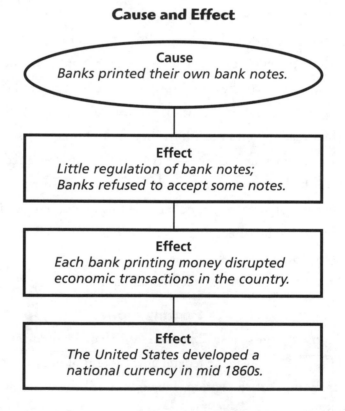

This type of graphic organizer is called a causal chain because it shows that one cause produced an effect, which, in turn produced another effect.

Problem and Solution

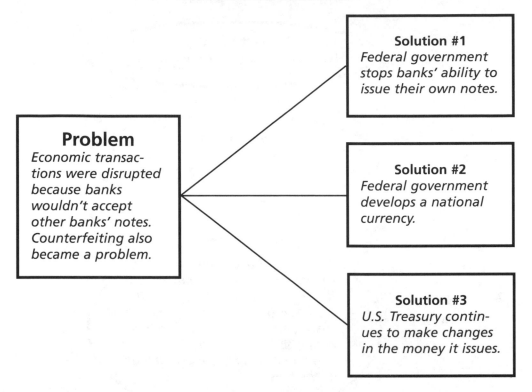

Problem
Economic transactions were disrupted because banks wouldn't accept other banks' notes. Counterfeiting also became a problem.

Solution #1
Federal government stops banks' ability to issue their own notes.

Solution #2
Federal government develops a national currency.

Solution #3
U.S. Treasury continues to make changes in the money it issues.

This graphic organizer shows that three steps were taken to eventually solve the problem and that one led to the other. The organizer also displays the idea of government action over time.

Compare and Contrast

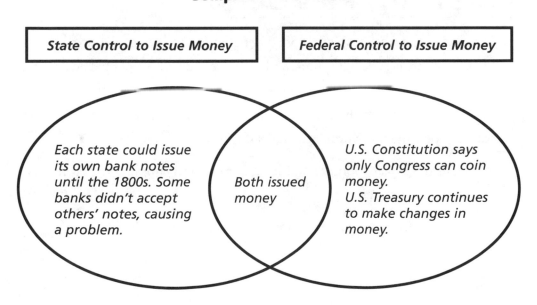

State Control to Issue Money

Federal Control to Issue Money

Each state could issue its own bank notes until the 1800s. Some banks didn't accept others' notes, causing a problem.

Both issued money

U.S. Constitution says only Congress can coin money.
U.S. Treasury continues to make changes in money.

Sequence or Chronological Order

```
        ┌──────────────────────────────┐
        │         First Event          │
        │  State banks issue their own │
        │            money.            │
        └──────────────────────────────┘
                      │
        ┌──────────────────────────────┐
        │          Next Event          │
        │  Some banks would not accept  │
        │  these notes, causing         │
        │  financial disruption.        │
        └──────────────────────────────┘
                      │
        ┌──────────────────────────────┐
        │          Last Event          │
        │  Federal government           │
        │  establishes the U.S.         │
        │  Treasury and a national      │
        │  currency. The Treasury       │
        │  continues to change the      │
        │  money, such as elimi-        │
        │  nating $500, $1,000, and     │
        │  $10,000 bills and changing   │
        │  the actual look of the bills.│
        └──────────────────────────────┘
```

Step 5: Students present the finished product to others in the class.

Using the Strategy in Your Classroom

Previewing the text is essential for students to get an idea of the text's "layout." It helps students get ready to think and organize their ideas in a particular way. If students have not had any previous experience with using graphic organizers, you may wish to introduce them a little at a time. Here are some tips for helping students become more proficient users of graphic organizers:

- Begin the explanation of graphic organizers with simple text that has an obvious structure.

- Present one graphic organization at a time.

- Then move into having students compare and contrast representations.

- Help students use signal or transition words to determine the structure of a text. These are words such as *for instance, similar to, different from,* and *because* that indicated how ideas are related in a text.

- Then have students use two, then three, then four types of organizers.

As students become more accustomed to discussing and using graphic organizers, they will be able to adapt them to both their purpose for reading and the type of text they are reading. Eventually, students should be able to generate graphic organizers on their own and use them in their notetaking.

Extending the Strategy

If students are using webbing in their reading or English/language arts class, be sure to help them make the connection that using graphic organizers in social studies is much the same process. This would also be a good time to talk to students about the differences in narrative and expository text. Occasionally, pieces of narrative text are inserted in social studies textbooks to elaborate on a point. Students can be shown the different functions of each type of text—graphic organizers are the perfect vehicle for achieving this goal.

Graphic organizers can also be used as a stimulus for writing expository essays. Students learning to compose essays in compare-and-contrast, chronological-sequence, problem-and-solution, or cause-and-effect patterns should capture their ideas in a graphic organizer before they begin writing.

As you can see, previewing the text is essential in deciding which graphic organizer is most appropriate. Therefore, you may wish to connect this strategy with Strategies 1 and 2.

Some Final Thoughts

Unfortunately, not all text is neatly packaged into the tidy structures I have presented so far. Sometimes, text does not follow a definite structure, and sometimes it changes from one structure to another in the same chapter. When this happens, it is wise to discuss the author's purpose for the text and help students construct their own way of organizing the ideas presented.

Practice the Strategy

Use these online materials to guide your students as they practice the Using Graphic Organizers strategy.

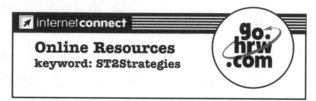

internet**connect**

Online Resources
keyword: ST2Strategies

go.
hrw
.com

Read More about It

Dye, G. A. 2000. Graphic organizers to the rescue! Helping students link—and remember—information. *Teaching Exceptional Children,* 32 (3), 72–76.

Irwin-DeVitis, L. & Pease, D. 1995. Using graphic organizers for learning and assessment in middle level classrooms. *Middle School Journal,* 26 (5), 57–64

Robinson, D. H. 1998. Graphic organizers as aids to text learning. *Reading Research and Instruction,* 37 (2), 85–105.

Strategy 4
Constructing Concept Maps

As you saw in Strategy 3, graphic organizers can help students visualize and make sense of expository text. One special type of graphic organizer we will focus on here is the concept map. A concept map, sometimes called a semantic map, allows students to zero in on the most important points of the text. The map is made up of lines, boxes, circles, and/or arrows. It can be as simple or as complex as students make it and as the text requires.

How Can the Strategy Help My Students?

When struggling readers begin reading a portion of a social studies text, they generally start reading at the beginning, get bogged down in the first three paragraphs because they are having difficulty with comprehension, and never really figure out what the text is about. They miss the most important points in the passage. The concept map is designed to help students focus on and organize these most noteworthy points in the text so that they can use them later for discussion, a writing assignment, or a test. When students preview a reading passage and then work through a reading assignment, they can arrange and rearrange important concepts as needed.

Getting Started

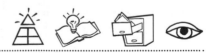

Previewing the text helps students see the structure of the entire passage. With a description-type structure, students may notice signal or transition words such as *for instance, for example, such as, in addition,* or *furthermore.* These signal words indicate that the text is describing or explaining important concepts. The following steps may be helpful in having students complete a concept map:

Step 1: Preview the Passage. Previewing can help students determine which kind of structure might be most appropriate to display the ideas in the text.

Step 2: Sketch a Concept Map. Looking at the boldfaced type, headings, and general structure of the text, students should sketch out a map to display the ideas in the passage.

Step 3: Read the Passage.

Step 4: Construct a Map. Using boxes, lines, arrows, bubbles, circles, or any other figure, students will display the ideas in the text in a concept map.

The Strategy in Action

The following steps show you how to implement the strategy. This activity is centered around the topic of erosion.

Step 1: Preview the Passage. Previewing can help a student determine a possible structure for the map. In this case, students may notice that the major concept is erosion and that the three subconcepts—water, glaciers, and wind—are the forces that cause erosion.

Step 2: Sketch a Concept Map. Students may look at the boldfaced type, headings, and general structure of the text and make their sketches. When students begin to sketch these concepts, they will quickly realize that water has the largest amount of text and the most terms to be defined. Putting water in the center may help students better display the ideas.

Step 3: Read the Passage.

Erosion

Another process of changing primary landforms into secondary landforms is **erosion**. Erosion is the movement of rocky materials to another location. Moving water is the most common force that erodes and shapes the land. In mountainous areas, streams cut into the land, forming steep, V-shaped valleys. Ravines and canyons are other examples of landforms created by flowing water.

Water. Flowing water carries sediment. This sediment forms different kinds of landforms depending on where it is deposited. For example, a river flowing from a mountain range onto a flat area, or plain, may deposit some of its sediment there. The sediment sometimes builds up into a fan-shaped form called an **alluvial fan.** Rivers create another type of landform when they flood their banks. The floodwaters deposit sediment, creating a landform called a **floodplain.** Rivers carry some of their sediment all the way to the ocean. A river's flow slows as it enters the ocean. The sediment then settles to the bottom. Some rivers create landforms called **deltas** where the river joins the ocean. The Nile and Mississippi Rivers have two of the world's largest deltas.

Waves in the ocean and in lakes also shape the land they touch. Waves can shape beaches into great dunes. Such dunes are found on the shore of Long Island and the central coast of California. The jagged coastline of Oregon also shows the erosive power of waves.

Glaciers. In high mountain settings and in the coldest places on Earth are **glaciers.** These large, slow-moving rivers of ice have the power to move tons of rock.

Giant sheets of thick ice called continental glaciers cover Greenland and Antarctica. Over the past 2 million years Earth has experienced several ice ages—periods of extremely cold conditions. During each ice age continental glaciers covered most of Canada and the northern United States. The Great Lakes were carved out by the movement of a continental glacier.

Wind. Wind also shapes the land. Strong winds can lift soils into the air and carry them across great distances. On beaches and in deserts wind can deposit large amounts of sand to form dunes.

Blowing sand can wear down rock. The sand acts like sandpaper to polish jagged edges. An example of rocks worn down by blowing sand can be seen in Utah's Canyonlands National Park.

Step 4: **Construct a Map.** Have students use boxes, lines, arrows, bubbles, circles, or any other figure to display the ideas in the text in a concept map. While Figure 4.1 looks somewhat complex, it simply represents the ideas presented in the text. If students understand the ideas presented in this concept map, they will most likely be able to use that information in writing a paper, taking a test, or discussing the topic with a friend.

Figure 4.1

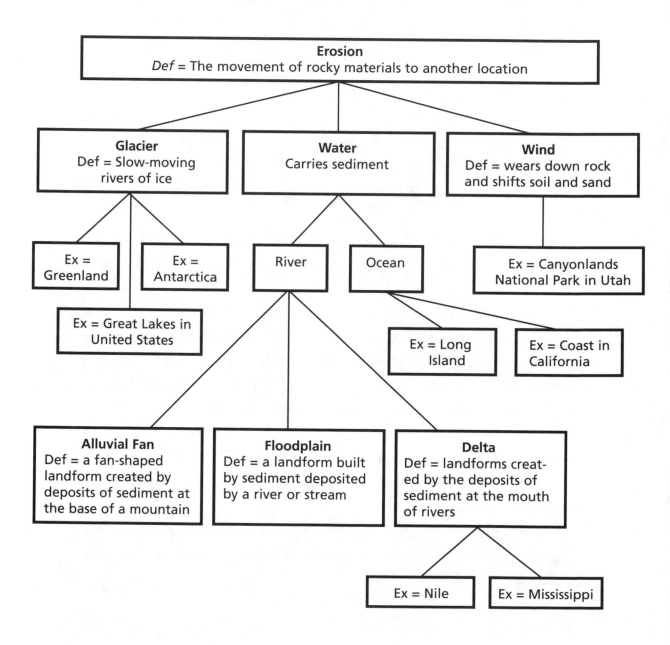

Using the Strategy in Your Classroom

When first introducing the concept map to students, you may wish to create most of the map yourself and have students complete it after they have used a pre-reading strategy and have read the text. The mapping strategy is most effective, however, if students create their own concept maps. Definitions and examples can be embedded within the maps to help remind students of the meaning of particular concepts. As students create their own maps, they should be directed to use headings, boldfaced type, and the way that text is organized to construct the maps.

Concept maps work best with text that explains one or more ideas and provides supporting examples. A concept map may be displayed hierarchically such as in Figure 4.1, or, a more free-form style, such as in Figure 4.2.

Figure 4.2

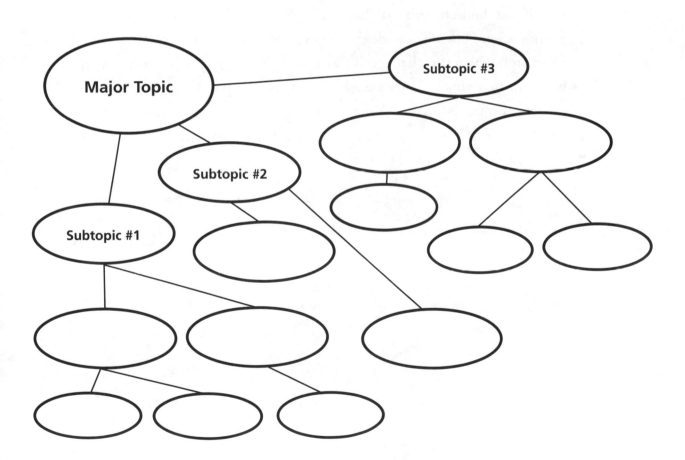

Any combination and any organization of circles, bubbles, squares, triangles, lines, or arrows can be used to construct a concept map. Previewing helps students see the overall picture. Sketching gives students an idea of how the key concepts can best be displayed. Constructing the final map helps students understand how the concepts relate to one another. Some teachers suggest sketching the ideas via "sticky" notes and then constructing the final concept map when students are satisfied with the display.

Extending the Strategy

Struggling readers may need more help to begin a task such as creating a concept map. A Cloze Concept Map may support such readers. After students complete a pre-reading strategy on the topic, you can give them an almost-completed map. Some of the boxes should be left blank and have bold lines around them, as shown in Figure 4.3 on the next page.

If you think students may have difficulty with this task, you may wish to provide a word box with the deleted items listed. As students become more and more proficient at completing this Cloze Concept Map, more boxes can be left blank. As time goes on, once students have finished a pre-reading strategy, you can give them a blank concept map to fill out as they read. Eventually, they should be able to construct their own maps after first previewing the text, and making a sketch and then filling it in as they read.

Figure 4.3

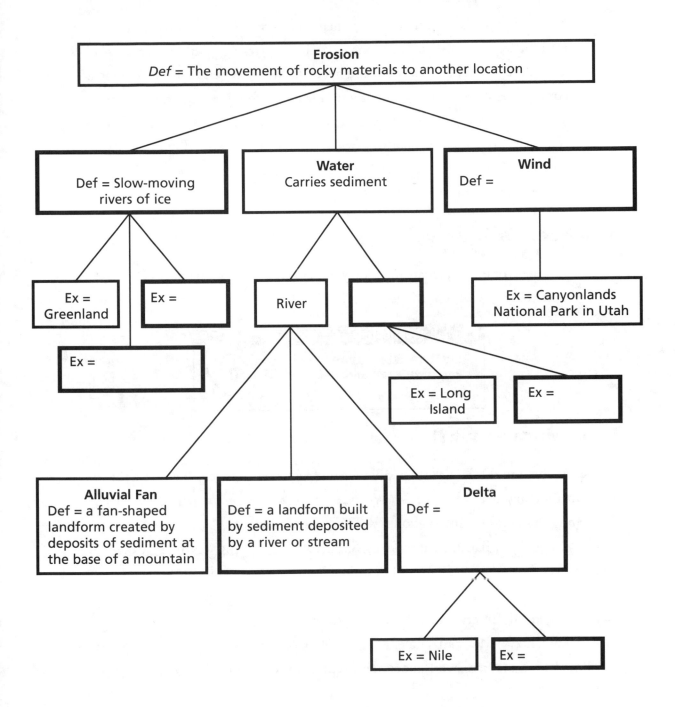

Some Final Thoughts

Not all text lends itself to a concept map, but most of the material your students read for social studies should work well with the strategy. After all, social studies is all about concepts, examples, and generalizations. When first introducing a concept map, use a short and fairly simple text before moving on to a more complex and longer one. Although sometimes a challenge, it is best to limit concept maps to one page. That way, when students go to study for a test or use the information in writing, the text's most important ideas are displayed in a handy and easy-to-use format.

Practice the Strategy

Use these online materials to guide your students as they practice the Constructing Concept Maps strategy.

internet **connect**

Online Resources
keyword: ST2Strategies

go.
hrw
.com

Read More about It

Alvermann, D. E. 1986. Graphic organizers: Cueing devices for comprehending and remembering main ideas. In *Teaching main idea comprehension,* edited by J. F. Baumann. Newark, DE: International Reading Association.

Avery, P. G., Baker, J., and Gross, S. H. 1997. "Mapping" learning at the secondary level. *The Clearing House,* 70 (5): 279–85.

Heimlich, E. and Pittleman, S. D. 1986. *Semantic mapping: Classroom applications.* Newark, DE: International Reading Association.

Romance, N. R., and Vitale, M. R. 1999. Concept mapping as a tool for learning: Broadening the framework for student-centered instruction. *College Teaching,* 47 (2): 74–79.

Strategy 5
Visualizing Information

Social studies textbooks are full of charts, diagrams, pictures, illustrations, political cartoons, and maps. These visual aids are placed in textbooks to enhance the learning of the content. In their rush to complete an assignment, students often skip over the visual information that may actually assist them in the comprehension process.

Struggling readers often have difficulty visualizing ideas presented in text. The Information Age has certainly bombarded students today with visual images. Some say that the beautiful picture books, the television, the Internet, CD–ROMs, and so forth may have taken away a student's need (and perhaps ability) to visualize. Others may argue that youth today "think" in visual images. Whatever the case, proficient readers visualize as they read—struggling readers generally do not.

How Can the Strategy Help My Students?

Visual information displayed in a social studies textbook can be flipped over and ignored or studied and incorporated. What students *do* with the visual information is the important ingredient to comprehending text. Rakes, Rakes, and Smith (1995) suggested that a teacher can help students use information on increasingly interactive levels. The teacher can:

1. Provide written or oral directions immediately before students "read" the visual information, such as "On this map, you will notice. . . ."

2. Direct students' attention through study questions to the important features accompanying visuals, such as "This chart displays the most common transportation in America during the Industrial Revolution. . . ."

3. Encourage students to evaluate the graphics in the text and think about how the graphics and text relate to one another. You might ask, "Given the most important point of this passage, is this graphic representative of. . . ."

4. Ask students to create their own visuals depicting the information represented in the text. When students draw a sketch or picture of the information in the text, they have made a connection between what they know and what they are reading. Illustrations can be used to summarize text, and graphic organizers and concept maps (Strategies 3 and 4) can assist students in integrating new knowledge with existing knowledge.

The more that students are involved in creating the visual image, the more engaged they will be with the ideas in the text. Depending on the purpose of the assigned reading, you may wish to direct students to visuals, have them evaluate the visual information presented, and/or have students create their own graphic representations of the ideas presented in the text.

Getting Started

Step 1: **Preview the Text, Noting the Visual Information Presented.** This information may be in the form of charts, diagrams, pictures, or illustrations.

Step 2: **Ask How the Visual Information Relates to the Text or Why the Author(s) Included This Information.** It is important that students create a link between the text and the visual. Having students use a transparency, you may wish to ask them to actually draw arrows between the text and the visual.

Step 3: **Generate Questions Raised by the Visual Aid.** Students should list two to three questions that arise from this visual aid.

Step 4: **Read the Text.**

Step 5: **Go Back and Review Visual Aids in the Text.** Students should evaluate whether the visual accurately displays the most important ideas in the text.

The Strategy in Action

The following steps show you how to implement the strategy. This activity is centered around the topic of nationalism.

Step 1: Preview the Text, Noting the Visual Information Presented. This may be charts, diagrams, pictures, or illustrations. Using the reading on nationalism, students should be directed to notice the political cartoon that accompanies the text. A quick preview will tell students that the major topic of the text is nationalism, and they should predict that the political cartoon (shown on the next page) will support that concept. The cartoon depicts five men trying to keep the pot labeled "Balkan Troubles" from boiling over. The caption indicates that the British were concerned with the Balkan situation.

Nationalism

During the 1800s **nationalism**—the feeling that a specific nation, language, or culture is superior to all others—had become a force for unification. In 1871 Kaiser Wilhelm I unified a number of German states into the German Empire. Later the Pan-German movement sought to unite most of the other German-speaking people in Europe under Germany.

Although nationalism helped to create and enlarge Germany, it threatened the stability of some nations. Austria-Hungary included people of many nationalities and languages. One of these groups, the Slavs, wanted to create a nation of their own. Serbia was already an independent Slavic country on the Balkan Peninsula. The Serbs encouraged Slavs within the Austro-Hungarian Empire to break free and join them in creating an independent, united Slavic empire in the Balkans. Russia, itself largely Slavic, supported Serbia's goal.

Austro-Hungarian leaders saw this movement as a threat to their authority. One Austrian official predicted that Slavic nationalism was "one of the powerful national movements which can neither be ignored nor kept down." The hostilities in the Balkan region grew so intense that many people referred to the Balkans as a "powder keg." The area seemed a likely place to ignite a major European war.

THE BOILING POINT

In this 1912 cartoon, British leaders try to keep trouble in the Balkans from boiling over.

Nawrocki Stock Photo

Step 2: **Ask How the Visual Information Relates to the Text or Why the Author(s) Included This Information.** It is important that students create a link between the text and the visual. If you put this reading on a transparency, students could actually draw an arrow between the text and the cartoon. Alternatively, some teachers place a blank transparency over the book pages and have students draw and arrow between the graphic and the appropriate text. Paragraph one in the reading provides an overview to the concept of nationalism. Paragraph two talks about Germany and then the Slavs. Paragraph three describes Slavic nationalism and clearly describes the cartoon.

Step 3: **Generate Questions Raised by the Visual Aid.** Students should list two to three questions that arise from this visual aid. Students may ask the following questions:

Who are the Slavs?

Where are the Balkans?

Why would the British be concerned about Balkan nationalism?

Step 4: **Read the Text.**

Step 5: **Go Back and Review Visual Aids in the Text.** After reading, students should connect the ideas in paragraph three with the information in the cartoon. They should now answer any questions they posed during the pre-reading period and perhaps add another, "What is the situation in the Balkans today?" They should now understand the concept of nationalism and how the Balkans are an example of this concept. They also should be able to explain how the political cartoon extends the meaning of the text.

Using the Strategy in Your Classroom

This strategy can, of course, be modified to suit the needs of your students and their purpose for reading. Based on Rakes, Rakes, and Smith's levels of interaction presented earlier, you could (1) simply direct students to notice the cartoon, (2) provide study questions based on the cartoon, (3) have students evaluate how well the cartoon helps them understand the text better, or (4) have students sketch their own understanding of nationalism. In addition, questions can direct students' understanding of how this concept fits with information presented before and after this text. A slightly different arrangement of this strategy would be used for other forms of visual information such as charts, diagrams, maps, or photographs.

Extending the Strategy

Some educators suggest that after reading, students be asked to draw the visual from memory. This works particularly well for diagrams explained in the text. The act of creating a graphic helps students process it better and connect to the information presented in the text. In addition, this activity can certainly be used to assess how well students understood the text.

Student-created graphics can be extended through group work by having students explain their graphic to other students. They benefit from hearing and seeing the various perspectives of other students. Without employing competition such as "whose graphic is the best?", students can be guided to give feedback on other students' graphics. Giving and soliciting feedback helps them process the ideas in the text more deeply and become better consumers of displays of visual information.

Some teachers have used a Visual Reading Guide (Stein, 1978) for many years. This study guide is simply constructed to direct students to preview the visual information in the text before they read, answering some preliminary questions before and after reading.

The graphic organizers and concept maps presented in Strategies 3 and 4 are additional ways of encouraging students to visualize and organize the ideas in the text. Some computer software allows students to flip between graphic representations and an outline of the material.

Some Final Thoughts

Not all text has visual information that is placed there strategically or is well explained and connected to the text in the caption. If this is the case, then having students evaluate and/or redraw graphics may be useful. Also, because of time constraints, a teacher can not give this type of attention to every visual aid in the text. But when the visual information does help students better understand the ideas presented in the text, this strategy can be most helpful. Most students—but especially struggling readers—can benefit from learning how to attend to and use the visual aids that often accompany social studies texts.

Practice the Strategy

Use these online materials to guide your students as they practice the Visualizing Information strategy.

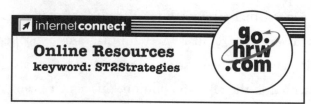

internet**connect**

Online Resources
keyword: ST2Strategies

go.
hrw
.com

Read More about It

Hyerle, D. 1996. *Visual tools for constructing knowledge.* Alexandria, VA: Association for Supervision and Curriculum Development.

Rakes, G. C., Rakes, T. A., and Smith, L. J. 1995. Using visuals to enhance secondary students' reading comprehension of expository text. *Journal of Adolescent and Adult Literacy,* 39 (1): 46–54.

Scevak, J., and Moore, P. 1997. The strategies students in years 5, 7, and 9 use for processing texts and visual aids. *The Australian Journal of Language and Literacy,* 20 (4): 280–88.

Stein, H. 1978. The visual reading guide (VRG). *Social Education,* 42 (6): 534–35.

Strategy 6
Building Background Information

Have you ever tried to read a computer manual or something else that was highly technical when you lacked the background knowledge to really understand it? It is very frustrating to read something on a topic you know very little about. Students encounter that feeling often when they attempt to read a social studies textbook. Fortunately, there is much you can do to help students build the information they need to be successful before beginning a reading assignment.

One strategy for achieving this goal is the Predicting and Confirming Activity (PACA). The activity is based on Beyer's (1971) inquiry model. Social studies teachers find this strategy very compatible with their content. The purpose of the strategy is to help build background information when students are going to read about something they know very little about so that when they approach the reading selection, they will be more successful and have a context for understand the ideas presented.

How Can the Strategy Help My Students?

Students often have no personal connection with much of what we hope they learn in social studies classrooms. They have a context for American history and geography, but often struggle with subjects such as world cultures. For students to learn anything new, they must connect it in some way to something they already know. Good teachers help students make the connection between new information and what they already know.

Getting Started

The Predicting and Confirming Activity uses student predictions to set a purpose for reading. Students make these predictions based on an initial set of information provided by the teacher. Given additional information, students can revise their predictions (or hypotheses) and pose them as questions to be answered during reading.

Step 1: **Provide Some Initial Information and Pose a General Question.** A word list and a question are usually enough to assist students in making predictions. But if they are not, you can couple the word list with a short overview of the topic.

Step 2: **Write Predictions Based on the Initial Information.** These predictions can be discussed and written on the chalkboard or written by individual students or groups of students.

Step 4: **Provide New Information.** This can be in the form of pictures, charts, diagrams, maps or other visual information from the textbook, a video, or from reading a story.

Step 5: **Review Predictions.** Students may revise, confirm, or reject their original predictions. Then they turn them into questions for reading. Based on the new information, students discuss—as a class or in small groups—which of their original predictions they want to keep and which they no longer think apply. They may also revise some predictions to be more accurate. They then turn these predictions into questions they want answered during reading.

Step 6: **Read the Text.**

Step 7: **Revisit Predictions and Answer Questions.** Students once again look at their predictions and answer the questions they generated earlier. From here, depending on the purpose of the reading, you may wish to ask students to write about their new learning, formulate study questions and answers, or use some graphic representation of their learning.

The Strategy in Action

The following steps show you how to implement the strategy. This activity centers around the topic of Hinduism. (The Predicting and Confirming Activity works best with content that is unfamiliar to students, such as world cultures, geography, or anthropology.)

Hinduism

Hinduism is one of the oldest major religions in the world today. Hindus worship many gods. These include Brahma the Creator, Vishnu the Preserver, and Siva the Destroyer. Hinduism teaches that all gods and all living beings are part of a single spirit.

Two important beliefs in Hinduism are reincarnation and karma. Reincarnation is the belief that the soul is reborn again and again in different forms. Karma is the positive or negative force caused by a person's actions. Hindus believe that a person with good karma may be reborn as a person of higher status. A person with bad karma may be reborn with lower status, or as an animal or insect.

Hinduism also teaches a special respect for cows. Hindus do not eat beef. Even today, cows can be seen roaming cities and villages.

Step 1: **Provide Some Initial Information and Pose a General Question.** Words on the list should contain the important concepts in the reading and then 10 to 15 more familiar terms that students will know. Based on the reading about Hinduism, the following words can be used to answer the question "What are the basic beliefs of Hinduism?"

reincarnation	Vishnu, the Preserver	insect
karma	animal	Siva, the Destroyer
cows	religion	village
Brahma, the Creator	soul	beef
spirit	positive force	belief
cities	reborn	gods
negative force	high status	

Step 2: **Write Predictions Based on the Initial Information.** These predictions can be discussed and written on the board or written by individual students or groups of students. Based on this initial information, students may make the following predictions:

Hindus believe that people have a positive or negative force.

Hindus think that people are reborn or reincarnated.

Brahma created all life.

Hindus may live in villages or cities.

All animals are important to Hindus.

People with a positive force have high status.

Hindus have lots of gods, not just one.

Step 4: **Provide New Information.** You should ask students to look at relevant pictures, such as images of an Indian town and of the god Siva, that they can find in their textbooks or other sources. However, since these visual aids may provide only limited information, you might want to fill in some details with a short story or additional pictures.

Step 5: **Review Predictions.** Going back to their original predictions, students may add some predictions such as "Cows are important to Hindus, because they wander the streets with people."

Step 6: **Read the Text.**

Step 7: **Revisit Predictions and Answer Questions.** At this point, students go back to their original predictions and see which ones may be revised or confirmed. They may also check to see if their questions were answered.

Using the Strategy in Your Classroom

The Predicting and Confirming Activity is simply a method for building background information before reading. When students read after completing this strategy, they will be able to connect what they are reading and what they now know about the topic. The predictions turned into questions help guide their reading as well.

When constructing the initial word list, it is important to include both words students will know and some they will encounter in the reading. While discussing these words in small groups in order to write their predictions, students may guess at the meanings of unknown words, or someone in the group may know the word.

If students do not know enough about the topic to even begin predicting, then you could start off with a reading or an overview of the topic or have students leaf through the textbook to get some ideas. You could also direct students to write a sentence using two or more words in the list to construct the prediction.

Extending the Strategy

After questions are formulated and predictions are made, you may wish to use a jigsaw design to complete the reading. Groups would be assigned to answer specific questions about the topic—each group forming an expert group. Then one student from each group would share his or her "expert" information with the base group to complete the synthesizing activity.

If students need additional help in processing new information, they could be asked to visualize. In the example above, they may be asked to describe what they would see when visiting a town where many Hindus live: what would they see, feel, smell, hear? They could also organize their newfound knowledge into a graphic organizer or employ a sketch or diagram. Additionally, they could extend and organize their thoughts by writing a summary or report.

Some Final Thoughts

What you risk when using a Predicting and Confirming Activity is that students may form misconceptions while making predictions based on limited information. Revisiting the predictions is an important part of this strategy because it is your opportunity to correct these misconceptions and expand on students' knowledge about the topic. For this reason, some teachers prefer to display the predictions through newsprint or overheads or by writing them on the chalkboard. A classroom environment in which students are free to guess and be wrong is an essential component to implementing this strategy.

Some pictures in books are rich with information and some are not. You may need to supplement the text with videos, pictures, or stories. The purpose is to build background information where none or little exists so that students can be more successful when they read their social studies textbooks. In the process, students may learn that making and confirming predictions is an essential part of effective reading.

Practice the Strategy

Use these online materials to guide your students as they practice the Building Background Information strategy.

internet **connect**

Online Resources
keyword: ST2Strategies

go.
hrw
.com

Read More about It

Beyer, B. K. 1971. *Inquiry in the social studies classroom.* Columbus, OH: Charles E. Merrill Publishing Company.

Harmon, J. M., Katims, D. S., and Whittington, D. 1999. Helping middle school students learn from social studies texts. *Teaching Exceptional Children* 32 (1): 70–75.

Nessell, D. 1988. Channeling knowledge for reading expository text. *Journal of Reading* 32 (3): 231–35.

Weir, C. 1998. Using embedded questions to jump-start metacognition in middle school remedial readers. *Journal of Adolescent and Adult Literacy* 41 (6): 458–68.

Strategy 7
Making Predictions

One of the most important strategies students can use when approaching a new reading assignment is making predictions. Hilda Taba (1967) was one of the first educators to suggest a method for encouraging even young children to think at higher levels. Her concept-formation model was later adapted as List-Group-Label, a strategy to activate what students know about a topic, build and expand on what they know, and organize that knowledge before they begin reading. Building on Taba's original work, reading educators later added the "map" step. This strategy can also be used as a diagnostic instrument to find out what students know about a subject before they read and as an organizational tool to facilitate higher-level thinking through making predictions. Because the strategy involves the categorization and labeling of words, List-Group-Label-Map also makes an excellent pre-reading strategy for a vocabulary development lesson.

How Can the Strategy Help My Students?

When students begin reading a social studies textbook without activating what they know first, they often miss the connections that would help them store that information in longer-term memory. In addition, many students lack the ability to categorize and classify information. This process of grouping concepts helps students understand the relationships between ideas. When students engage in classifying and categorizing concepts before they read, it helps them connect to what they already know about a topic and better understand the concepts when they read about them. Creating a concept map before reading gives students the opportunity to "see" the ideas and their relationships while reading.

Getting Started

The List-Group-Label-Map strategy works best when students already know something about a topic. During the initial discussion, teachers may ascertain how much students already know about a topic and correct any misconceptions they may have.

Step 1: **Make a Word List.** Students are directed to an initial piece of information and asked to list as many words related to the topic as possible. Pictures are the best and easiest stimulus for students to come up with a list of words, although other visual information in the textbook can be used. These words may be associations they come up with from memory if the topic is very familiar. Many teachers also use videos to elicit the words. If you conduct the discussion with the entire class, write the word lists in columns on the chalkboard or on an overhead transparency. If the discussion occurs within a small group, a student can record the words.

Step 2: **Look for Word Associations.** Students group items by indicating which words belong together. Only one student in a group should indicate which words go together. The teacher (or student in a group) then marks the words with an *X* or *O* or some other symbol. If another student wants to add to the grouping, it is important that the first student be consulted because he or she may be thinking of a different category. Students can use words more than once.

Step 3: **Label Word Groups.** Then the student who came up with the original groupings goes back and labels each group. These labels actually represent concepts, and the words are then examples of these concepts.

Step 4: **Make a Concept Map.** Individually or in small groups, students use the words listed to create concept maps, following the process described in Strategy 4.

Step 5: **Read the Text.**

Step 6: **Revisit the Concept Map.** Students go back and take another look at the map, adding information from the reading. During reading, students may note whether the map they created was consistent with the ideas presented in the text. After reading, students elaborate on their maps using the ideas in the text. This expanded map connects what they knew before reading with what they learned about the topic.

The Strategy in Action

The following steps show you how to implement the strategy. This activity centers around the topic of western settlement in the 1800s. (You will notice that this activity is very similar to the topic covered in Strategy 2: Understanding Text. You could combine these two strategies and have students make predictions and look at the text's structure at the same time.)

Home in the Desert

TURNING A RIVER.

Western settlers used crude machinery to dam rivers during the 1800s. Their efforts required extensive labor. Culver Pictures, Inc.

One of the most important tasks the Mormons faced was turning the desert into their Promised Land. Shortly after arriving at the Great Salt Lake, the Mormons dammed one of the streams that came down from the mountains to irrigate the soil and plant their first corps. Brigham Young established a new code regulating water rights.

In the East, water-use laws were intended to protect every person's access to this precious and necessary resource. Laws commonly required owners whose land bordered streams or rivers to maintain a free flow of water downstream. Specifically, such rules stated that landowners could not increase or decrease the flow of water or change its direction. These restrictions prevented landowners from constructing dams.

In the generally dry climate of the West, large-scale agriculture was not possible without irrigation. Settlers needed dams and canals to channel the scarce supplies of water to the fields. This need led the Mormons to develop a new water-use code. Under the Mormons' new code, the first person to use the water had full rights to its use. However, the water had to be used for beneficial purposes, such as farming, mining, or manufacturing. Mormon leaders allowed farmers, miners, or businesspeople only enough water to properly accomplish their tasks. They could not waste water. In any dispute over water use, the good of the community would outweigh the interests of individuals.

Young's words of welcome to new settlers expressed the Mormons' belief in cooperating to make the best use of their scarce resources:

> "[T]here shall be no private ownership of the streams that come out of the canyons, nor the timber that grows on the hills. These belong to the people: all the people."

Young's new approach helped the Mormons make the desert bloom with crops. It also created the basis for modern water-rights laws throughout the western United States.

Step 1: Make a Word List. Have students focus on the picture of the dam construction and ask them what they see in the picture. They should not analyze what they see, just describe at this point. Words that may be associated with the picture include:

dam	smoke	mountains	shovels	houses
men	trees	sky	hats	bushes
wheelbarrows	wood	barrels	rocks	planks
desert	wall	digging	brace	round things
water	pit	pulleys	tents	hole

Step 2: **Look for Word Associations.** It is important that only one student indicate which words go together in a group. You (or one student in a group) then marks the words with symbols, such as the ones shown below. If another student wants to add to a word list, make sure that the student talks his or her suggestion over with the first student. Remember that words can be used more than once. A sample grouping may look like this:

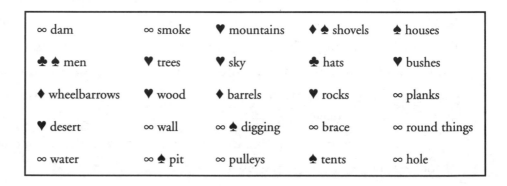

∞ dam	∞ smoke	♥ mountains	♦ ♠ shovels	♠ houses
♣ ♠ men	♥ trees	♥ sky	♣ hats	♥ bushes
♦ wheelbarrows	♥ wood	♦ barrels	♥ rocks	∞ planks
♥ desert	∞ wall	∞ ♠ digging	∞ brace	∞ round things
∞ water	∞ ♠ pit	∞ pulleys	♠ tents	∞ hole

Step 3: **Label Word Groups.** Students who came up with the original groupings should now go back and label each group. Here are some possible categories:

> ∞ = building the dam
> ↔ = appearance of men
> ♣ = tools or equipment
> ♦ = scenery or natural environment
> ♥ = living quarters
> ♠ = moving dirt

Step 4: **Make a Concept Map.** Individually or in small groups, students use the words listed to create a concept map like this one:

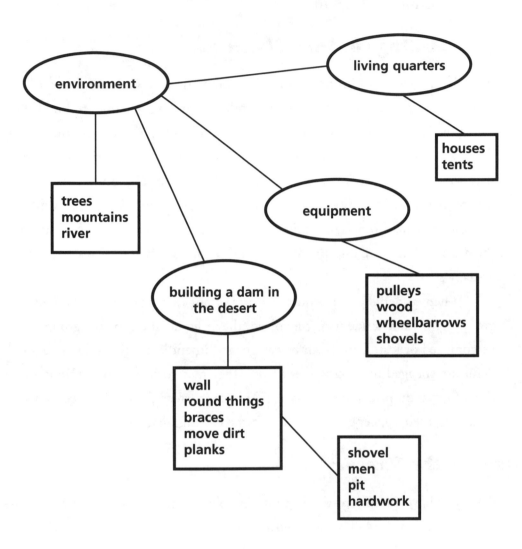

Step 5: **Read the Text.** After going through the List-Group-Label-Map process and studying the picture, students can then appreciate how scarce water was for the Mormons and why they had to work together as a community to preserve it.

Step 6: **Revisit the Concept Map.** During reading, students may note whether the map they created was consistent with the ideas presented in the text. After reading, encourage students to elaborate on their maps, using the ideas in the text. These expanded maps connect what students knew with what they learned about the topic. The maps may include ideas from the text, such as "land use laws," "used to irrigate farms," and so forth.

Using the Strategy in Your Classroom

Any picture, video, or initial information can be used to generate the word list. Pictures that give a lot of information work best and can be used to build the background information necessary to understand the text. Pictures also help students visualize what they read. To get students started, simply ask them what they see in the picture (or remember from the video, or saw on the way to school that morning). Since the next step is to classify and categorize words, discourage students from saying things like "creating a water source" or "changing the desert." These are interpretations from the picture rather than what they actually see.

When students group words, it is important that one person state his or her grouping. If more students get involved, the original labels for the groups may be confused or lost. Words can be categorized in endless ways. Whenever students are engaged in making predictions, they may form misconceptions about the information presented in the text. You can correct these misconceptions by reviewing their concept maps or during the ensuing discussion.

Extending the Strategy

After you have completed the List-Group-Label-Map process, you may wish to try any or all of the following extensions to the strategy.

Possible Sentences. Students connect two or more words from the list and write sentences inferring what the text will be about. These sentences can be formulated into a paragraph, and students can compare their predictions or use the word list to create a summary of what they have learned.

Writing Summaries. Using the list and the concept map, students can write a summary of the information after reading. Most students have difficulty writing summaries—a visual display of the ideas and words in a list can assist students in the process.

Comparing and Contrasting. Hilda Taba suggested that students be led to compare and contrast one piece of information with another and then be led, through carefully designed questions, to make a generalization using both sets of information.

List-Group-Label-Map lends itself well for combining with other strategies such as Understanding Text (Strategy 2). Depending on the needs of your students, how familiar they are with the topic, your instructional objectives, and the purpose for the reading, many of the strategies presented in this book can be used to support one another.

Some Final Thoughts

The List-Group-Label-Map strategy can be used by itself to generate information and inferences about a text before reading it, or it can be used with other strategies to extend student thinking and assist them in summarizing and making predictions. It is a simple flexible strategy that can be easily modified to meet your instructional goals. The strategy is a vehicle for using the wonderful visual information generally displayed in social studies textbooks to connect readers with text.

Practice the Strategy

Use these online materials to guide your students as they practice the Making Predictions strategy.

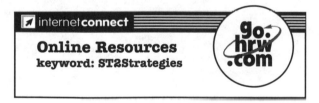

Read More about It

Blevins, W. 1990. Strategies for struggling readers: Making predictions. *Instructor* 108 (2): 49.

Caverly, D. C., Mandeville, T. F., and Nicholson, S. A. 1995. PLAN: A study-reading strategy for informational text. *Journal of Adolescent and Adult Literacy* 39 (3): 190–99.

Foley, C. L. 1993. Prediction: A valuable reading strategy. *Reading Improvement* 30 (3): 166–70.

Nolan, T. E. 1991. Self-questioning and prediction: Combining metacognitive strategies. *Journal of Reading* 35 (2): 132–38.

Stahl, S. A. and Kapinus, B. A. 1991. Possible sentences: Predicting word meanings to teach content area vocabulary. *Reading Teacher* (5)1: 36–43

Taba, H. 1967. *Teacher's Handbook for Elementary Social Studies.* Reading, MA: Addison-Wesley.

Strategy 8
Activating and Using Prior Knowledge

Strong readers know that asking questions and thinking about ideas while reading helps them understand and remember text. Students who begin reading a text with no preparation and no thought about the topic at hand can often complete an assignment but do not seem to remember much about what they read. One useful method for helping students over this hurdle is the KWL strategy, which was developed by Donna Ogle in 1986 and further refined by Carr and Ogle (1987). KWL stands for What I *K*now, What I *W*ant to Know, and What I *L*earned. The major purpose of this strategy is to activate students' prior knowledge:

BEFORE they read, by adding to that background information and assisting students in monitoring their learning

DURING reading by thinking about what they wanted to know or the questions they want answered about the topic, and

AFTER their reading by helping students to organize what they know through listing the things they learned about the topic.

The KWL chart looks like this:

What I Know	What I Want to Know	What I Learned

How Can the Strategy Help My Students?

Even when students possess prior knowledge about a topic, they do not tend to use that knowledge when they read unless it is "activated." The process is much like opening a file folder and reading the contents before attending a meeting. This review of prior knowledge gives you a frame of reference and helps you set a purpose for the meeting. Likewise, the KWL helps students review what they know about a topic, set a purpose for reading through what they want to know, and organize what they learned after reading.

For students who struggle when reading text, extra support can be given by the teacher or other students helping them study the charts, diagrams, maps, and pictures in the book to make some inferences or guesses about the topic. In addition, nonproficient and second-language learners can gain background information by listening to the discussion of others.

Getting Started

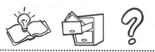

The KWL activity is most successful when students know something about the material but need to build on what they know to comprehend the text. Students can complete the KWL activity individually, in a small group, or as part of a whole class discussion. Struggling or second language learners may need the group or class discussion to build background knowledge where none exists.

Step 1: **Fill Out the First Two Columns of the KWL Chart.** That is, students should write down everything they *k*now for sure about the topic. Then they should write down everything they *w*ant to know about this topic in the middle column. Students are identifying what they know for sure and what they think they know about a topic. There is no set of correct answers, but misconceptions or wrong information can be flagged for further discussion. What they want to know should be phrased as questions.

Step 2: **Read, View, and/or Listen to Content about the Topic.**

Step 3: **Fill Out the Learned Column.** Students should work in a small group to elaborate on their answers.

Step 4: **Construct a Concept Map.** This map represents an integration of what students knew before reading and what they learned.

Step 5: Write a Summary. Using the concept map, students can move to writing a summary of what they learned about the subject. By writing the summary, students are engaged in focusing on the most important points in the reading.

The Strategy in Action

The following steps show you how to implement the strategy. This activity is centered around the topic of forecasting earthquakes.

Step 1: Fill Out the First Two Columns of the KWL Chart. Either individually, in small cooperative groups, or as an entire class students should fill out the first two columns of the KWL chart. Students write down everything they *know* for sure about the forecasting of earthquakes. Once they have finished, students write down everything they *want* to know about the topic in the middle column. Students are identifying what they know for sure and what they think they know about how scientists forecast earthquakes. At this point, you may want to note students' misconceptions or wrong information about the topic as a springboard for further discussion. Be sure to have students phrase what they want to know in column two as questions. If students lack prior knowledge about forecasting earthquakes, then they can look at pictures, charts, or diagrams in a textbook or other sources. Since this topic is quite narrow, you may wish to begin with what students know about earthquakes in general and move to the more specific topic of forecasting earthquakes.

Forecasting Earthquakes

What I Know	What I Want to Know	What I Learned
Some people know how to do it. Earthquakes don't always happen when you think they will. It is a science. It is hard to tell what the forces will be.	What equipment do they use? What do scientists know that helps them predict an earthquake? How far ahead of time can they predict an earthquake?	

Step 2: Read, View, and/or Listen to Content about the Topic.

Forecasting Earthquakes

Since ancient times, people have tried to forecast earthquakes. A Chinese inventor even created a device to register earthquakes as early as A.D. 132.

The theory of plate tectonics gives modern-day scientists a better understanding of how and why earthquakes occur. Earthquake scientists, known as seismologists, have many tools to help them monitor movements in Earth's crust. They try to understand when and where earthquakes will occur.

The most common of these devices is the seismograph. It measures seismic waves—vibrations produced when two tectonic plates grind against each other. Scientists believe that an increase in seismic activity may signal a coming earthquake.

Other devices show shifts in Earth's crust. Tiltmeters measure the rise of tectonic plates along a fault line. Gravimeters record changes in gravitational strength caused by rising or falling land. Laser beams can detect lateral movements along a fault line. Satellites can note the movement of entire tectonic plates.

Scientists have yet to learn how to forecast earthquakes with accuracy. Nevertheless, their ongoing work may one day provide important breakthroughs in the science of earthquake forecasting.

Step 3: Fill Out the Learned Column. Students would now fill out the Learned column based on what they just read.

Forecasting Earthquakes

What I Know	What I Want to Know	What I Learned
Some people know how to do it. Earthquakes don't always happen when you think they will. It is a science. It is hard to tell what the forces will be.	What equipment do they use? What do scientists know that helps them predict an earthquake? How far ahead of time can they predict an earthquake?	Chinese tried to predict earthquakes in A.D. 132 Theory of plate tectonics helps scientists today. Earthquake scientists are called seismologists Machine called seismograph Seismograph measures vibrations in two tectonic plates grinding against each other—this action may signal an earthquake. Tiltmeters measure the rise of tectonic plates. Gravimeters record changes in gravitational strength. Laser beams detect lateral movements along a fault line. Satellites note movement of entire plates. Scientists cannot yet predict earthquakes with accuracy.

Step 4: **Construct a Concept Map.** Students use the concept mapping technique to organize what they have learned about forecasting earthquakes. Student maps might look like this one.

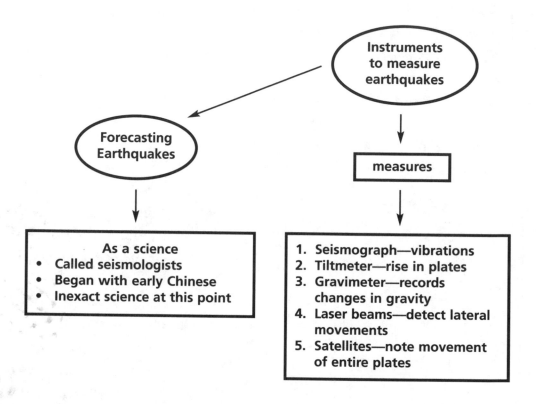

Step 5: **Write a Summary.** At this point students should be able to write a brief summary of the topic. A student summary might look like this:

Although scientists have tried to predict when an earthquake would hit for many years, they still cannot depend on their predictions at this point. These scientists, called seismologists, use many devices to forecast earthquakes. The most common is the seismograph, which measures the vibrations when two of Earth's plates grind against each other. Other instruments they use are the tiltmeter, gravimeter, laser beams, and satellites.

Using the Strategy in Your Classroom

The KWL strategy works best with topics about which students have some prior knowledge. If they know very little about a topic, students will have trouble filling in the first two columns of the chart. The purpose of the strategy is to *activate* what students know about a topic and, through discussion and further learning, *build background information.* If students are unsure how to identify what they know, perhaps they can scan their text or other resource they will be reading and make questions from subheadings to fill in this column. If the topic is too broad and students know a lot about it, they may get bogged down making a list. Sometimes you will not know how much prior knowledge students have until the brainstorming begins. To solve this problem, you might instruct your students to simply switch to creating a concept map first, so that they can organize their thoughts about the topic. Then have them summarize the key points in the What I Know column.

Another possibility is that when you ask students what they want to know, they will respond "nothing." For that reason, I like to refer to the middle column as "what you *think* you know." That way, students are making a choice between what they know for sure and the more tentative or acquainted knowledge of what they think they know. These statements of what they think they know can then be turned into questions they want answered in the reading.

Extending the Strategy

Because KWL is such a popular strategy, teachers have devised numerous variations to use it for different purposes with students. KWLs have been used successfully in primary, intermediate, middle, and high school classrooms as well as college courses. Instructions and assistance offered by teachers varies according to the age and experience of students.

One variation, known as WIKA, was developed by Richardson and Morgan (2000). WIKA stands for *What I Know Activity.* Some teachers find that the original format for KWL does not fit into the before-during-after framework, which is more clearly identified in the WIKA.

In this variation, the before-during-after instructional framework is clearly identified above the five columns.

- **What I already know** and **what I'd like to know** parallel the before-reading stage and are to be done before any reading on the topic occurs.

- **Interesting and/or important concepts from my reading** parallels the during-reading stage and is to be completed as the student reads. (This becomes a good place for notes and ongoing comprehension.)

- **What I know now** and **What I still want to know** parallel the after-reading stage so that students are encouraged to summarize, reflect, and anticipate new learning.

WIKA

Before Reading		During Reading	After Reading	
What I Already know	What I'd Like to Know	Interesting or Important Concepts from the Reading	What I Know Now	What I'd Still Like to Know

Other teachers have used these variations:

KWHL

What I *Know*	What I *Want* to Know	*How* I Will Find Out	What I *Learned*

Or:

KWLS

What I *Know*	What I *Want to* Know	What I *Learned*	What I *Still* Want to Learn

Some Final Thoughts

Feel free to modify the KWL strategy for your topic and the special needs of your students. If your students need more help thinking of what they know about a topic, you can show them a video, bring some pictures to class, have them leaf through their textbook, or perhaps read them a story. The first time you use any strategy, you will want to pick an easy text and keep the directions clear and simple. As students become more proficient using the strategy, more difficult text and variations may be used.

Some teachers are frustrated using a KWL because it takes longer to get "through" content. Keep in mind, however, that students tend to retain the information longer. True, it takes some time for students to understand the steps of a KWL, but, the purpose is to get them in the habit of thinking of what they know about a topic before they start reading.

Practice the Strategy

Use these online materials to guide your students as they practice the Activating and Using Prior Knowledge strategy.

internet**connect**

Online Resources
keyword: ST2Strategies

go.
hrw
.com

Read More about It

Bryan, J. 1998. K-W-W-L: Questioning the known. *The Reading Teacher* 51 (1): 618–20.

Cantrell, J. 1997. K-W-L leaning journals: A way to encourage reflection. *Journal of Adolescent and Adolescent Literacy* 40 (5): 392–93.

Carr, E. and Ogle, D. 1987. K-W-L Plus: A strategy for comprehension and summarization. *Journal of Reading,* 30 (7): 626–31.

Heller, M. 1986. How do you know what you know? Metacognitive modeling in the content areas. *Journal of Reading,* 29 (5): 415–22.

Huffman, L. E. 1998. Spotlighting specifics by combining focus questions with K-W-L. *Journal of Adolescent and Adolescent Literacy* 41 (6): 470–72.

Ogle, D. 1986. K-W-L: A teaching model that develops active reading of expository text. *The Reading Teacher,* 39 (6): 564–70.

Richardson, J. S. and Morgan, R. F. 2000. *Reading to learn in the content areas.* Belmont, CA:

Strategy 9
Anticipating Information

Anticipating what a text is going to be about helps readers connect the text with what they already know about a topic. Activating and using prior knowledge is an essential component of comprehending text. A strategy known as the Anticipation Guide was developed by Harold Herber in the early 1970s and has been used and modified over the years. The strategy is particularly well suited to teaching social studies content and helping students clarify their opinions and ideas about a topic.

How Can the Strategy Help My Students?

Middle and high school students love to debate, discuss, and voice their opinions. The Anticipation Guide uses this natural tendency to connect the ideas in a text with students' experience and knowledge. The purpose of the Anticipation Guide is to help students activate knowledge about a topic by voicing an opinion before they read, to focus their attention on the major points during their reading, and to provide a structure for discussing the text after they read. As students state their opinions about a text's topic, they tend to become more engaged and invested in supporting their viewpoint. This discussion alerts them to the important ideas in the text. In addition, students have a structure for discussing these ideas, and teachers can ask additional questions or make comments that expand student thinking.

Anticipation Guides work best with material that prompts students to form an opinion. For example, one teacher started a unit on comparative governments with this statement: "It is fair that some people make more money than others." The impending discussion on either side helped students understand socialist and democratic philosophies before reading about them. The steps of an Anticipation Guide are as follows:

Step 1: **Identify the Major Concepts.** Before students begin the activity, determine the main ideas of the reading selection, lecture, or film and write several statements that focus on the main points in the text and draw on students' backgrounds. Four to six statements are usually adequate to generate discussion.

Step 2: **Identify Agree/Disagree Statements.** Students point out statements with which they agree or disagree (write *agree* or *disagree* in column A). Rather than analyzing too much or second guessing, students should merely respond to the statements. Students respond individually—either negatively or positively—to each statement and can then compare responses in small groups.

Step 3: **Engage in Prereading Discussion.** You may wish to get a hand count of responses and ask students to justify their positions. Then engage students in a discussion of each statement's pros and cons.

Step 4: **Read the Text.** Students should be directed to look either for ideas that support or contradict the statements they just discussed.

Step 5: **Revisit the Statements**. Students should look at the statements they chose earlier to see if they have changed their opinions (write *agree* or *disagree* in column B). The purpose of this strategy is not to engage students in competition to see who is right or wrong, but rather to activate their opinions about issues that are related to the text and expand their thinking.

Step 6: **Engage in Postreading Discussion.** Looking again at the statements, students should compare their before-reading reactions to their after-reading reactions. Ask them to justify their new or continuing beliefs based on the reading.

The Strategy in Action

The following steps show you how to implement the strategy. This activity centers around the issues of women's rights.

Defending the Equal Rights Amendment

The U.S. Civil Rights Commission was established in 1957 to study issues involving discrimination. In 1978 the commission published a statement in support of the Equal Rights Amendment (ERA).

Ratification of the Equal Rights Amendment continues to be essential to the attainment [fulfillment] of equal rights for women and men under the law. In Federal statutes [laws] alone, the Commission had identified over 800 sections of the U.S. Code containing examples of . . . sex bias . . . that are inconsistent with a national commitment to equal rights, responsibilities, and opportunities. State laws are replete [filled] with provisions [conditions] that assign women on the basis of their sex, to an inferior role.

Measured by any standard, women continue to be disadvantaged by gender-based laws and practices, despite the enactment [passage] of equal opportunity laws. As workers, they are victims of an earnings gap that is even wider today than it was in 1956. As wives, they are still subject to laws that deny them an equal partnership in marriage. As students, they are often steered away from both the education needed to break into the better paying jobs dominated by men and the sports programs that have been traditional training grounds for leadership and the route to a college education through scholarships. Further, women endure [face] a criminal justice system that too often judges them by their sex and not by the acts they commit or by which they are victimized. This reality must dispel [end] the myth that women have achieved equality under the law.

It is clear that existing constitutional guarantees will not mandate [make] the changes that are needed. The Supreme Court has persisted [continued] in its view that sex-based laws and classifications are more easily justified under the Constitution than are race-based laws. . . . The treatment of challenges to sex-based discrimination under existing law reflects the perpetuation [continuation] of stereotypes and myths about women in American society, as well as a failure to recognize and understand the lengthy struggle of women in secure equal rights under the law.

Thus, the need for the Equal Rights Amendment to signal that sex discrimination is no longer acceptable in our Nation's laws, policies, and practices is even more clear today than it was in 1972 when Congress first approved the amendment and sent it to the States for ratification. . . . Recent experiences under State equal rights provisions [laws] . . . similar to the Federal ERA have confirmed that it will prompt the changes necessary to provide men and women with status as equal persons under the law.

Although these State experiences also suggest that reform is possible on a State-by-State basis, such a route is both plodding [slow] and haphazard [hit-or-miss] and offers no guarantees of ever reaching completion. As Congress recognized in 1972, "only a constitutional amendment can provide the legal and practical basis for the necessary changes." The ERA will provide on a national basis an unmistakable mandate [ruling] of the highest order for equal rights under the law. . . .

The Commission believes that the Equal Rights Amendment should be ratified. Accordingly, we urge State legislatures that have not yet approved the ERA to consider it on its merits. We are confident that such consideration can only result in ratification and the long-awaited guarantee to women and men of equal justice under the law.

From: *Statement on the Equal Rights Amendment,* United States Commission on Civil Rights, 1978.

Step 1: **Identify the Major Concepts.** The main idea of this reading is women's rights in the United States in the 1970s. Students should be directed to consider the statements and decide if they agree or disagree. The left column of the chart is for before reading and the right column is for after reading. The following statements can be used to stimulate discussion:

A Before Reading Agree/Disagree		B After Reading Agree/Disagree
	All men are created equal.	
	The law has traditionally favored men.	
	A woman's place is in the home.	
	The government should intervene if woman are not treated equally with men.	
	Women have fewer opportunities than men.	

Step 2: **Identify Agree/Disagree Statements.** Students should react generally to the statements because they do not yet have a context for them. Once students have looked at the statements, they should mark their choices in column A.

Step 3: **Engage in Prereading Discussion.** You may wish for students to compare answers within a small group before moving to a large group discussion. A hand count of answers before the discussion allows students to see how their opinions compare with those of other students. Students should be encouraged to give reasons or evidence for their opinions.

Step 3: **Read the Text.** Direct students to notice particularly any information that relates to the statements as they read the selection.

Step 4: **Revisit the Statements.** At this point, you need to see whether students have changed their minds about the statements. They should mark their new choices in column B. Students should be encouraged to change their opinions if the evidence in the text leads them to do so. Now would be a good time to talk about how opinions are often contextual. In 1776 when Thomas Jefferson wrote, "All men are created equal" in the Declaration of Independence, woman were not considered to be equal with men. If this statement were written today, it would read "All persons are created equal."

Step 5: **Engage in Postreading Discussion.** Students should now compare their before-reading responses with their after-reading responses. The discussion will now be centered on the Equal Rights Amendment and why this amendment was so hotly debated. You may wish to draw a parallel between the struggle for women's rights and the African Americans civil rights movement.

Using the Strategy in Your Classroom

The challenge in designing an Anticipation Guide is creating statements rather than questions, which may signal students that there is a right or wrong answer. The statements also need to connect what students already know with the major ideas in the text. In a sense, the statements represent the "so what" of the reading; that is, how does this selection relate to the lives of the students.

Duffelmeyer (1994) maintained that effective statements

- convey a sense of the major ideas that the student will encounter.

- activate and draw upon the students' prior experience.

- are general rather than specific.

- challenge students' beliefs.

After reading, students may wish to add to the statements or modify them in some way. The statements can be the basis for a writing assignment or an essay answer for a test.

Extending the Strategy

Writing assignments are a natural extension of the Anticipation Guide. Writing a persuasive essay is a requirement of many standardized tests. Students could be encouraged to take one or two of the statements, document them with evidence found in the text, and construct a persuasive essay. You may wish to work with an English/language arts teacher on this assignment.

As students get more proficient at using an Anticipation Guide, you can include some distracter statements that have little to do with the content. Critical readers can detect irrelevant comments as not central to the main argument. For students who are not yet ready to read this critically, these statements can be discussed after the reading.

Some Final Thoughts

While exchanging information with their classmates, it is easy for students to form misconceptions. It is particularly important during the prereading and postreading discussion, that you correct these misconceptions. Creating a classroom environment where students are free to make predictions and venture an opinion is the key to stimulating discussions. But monitoring those discussions is also an important role of the teacher.

The Anticipation Guide is an excellent method for promoting active reading, directing students' attention to the major points in the text, and helping them modify erroneous beliefs based on evidence. Using the natural propensity of adolescents to debate and argue, engages them in the content by connecting the topic to their lives.

Practice the Strategy

Use these online materials to guide your students as they practice the Anticipating Information strategy.

internet**connect**

Online Resources
keyword: ST2Strategies

go.
hrw
.com

Read More about It

Conley, M. 1985. Promoting cross-cultural understanding through content area reading strategies. *Journal of Reading* 28 (7): 600–05.

Duffelmeyer, F. A. 1994. Effective anticipation guide statements for learning from expository prose. *Journal of Reading* 37 (6): 452–57.

Erikson, B., Huber, M., Bea, T., Smith, C., and McKenzie, V. 1987. Increasing critical reading in junior high classes. *Journal of Reading* 30 (5): 430–39.

Herber, H. L. 1978. *Teaching reading in content areas.* Englewood Cliffs, NJ: Prentice-Hall.

Merkley, D. J. 1996–97. Modified anticipation guide. *Reading Teacher* 50 (4): 365–68.

Strategy 10

Developing Vocabulary Knowledge

All readers encounter words they do not know—strong readers have strategies for figuring out what to do with them. Strong readers use any or all of the following strategies when they encounter an unknown word:

- Skip it and read on

- Reread

- Think about what they are reading

- Sound it out to see if it is a word they have heard before

- Look at the headings and subheadings of the text

- Guess at what type of word would go there, such as a noun or an adjective

- Associate the parts of the word (prefixes, root words, suffixes) with words they know

I sometimes ask students this question: "When you are reading and you get stuck, what do you do?" Struggling readers generally respond by saying that they try sounding out the unfamiliar word, asking someone, or looking it up in the dictionary. In my opinion, it is better to teach students what strategies to use when they encounter an unknown word than it is to teach them a whole host of words in isolation. If they don't use these words in writing or see them in reading, students tend to forget them after the weekly vocabulary test.

Contextual Redefinition is a strategy that helps students acquire the ability to use context and structural analysis to figure out the meanings of unknown words. One important element in this strategy is the teacher modeling or thinking out loud about how to figure out the meaning of the word. This can be done by sharing the associations that come to mind when using structural analysis.

How Can the Strategy Help My Students?

Structural or morphemic analysis simply means associating the prefixes, root words, and suffixes with other meaningful word parts. Structural analysis is often taught in isolation and in English/language arts classes. When applied to social studies reading, structural analysis can be paired with contextual analysis. Together these techniques create a very powerful strategy for figuring out the meanings of unknown words.

Context present at the sentence level is not always helpful. The larger context of the entire passage or the paragraph should be used. Questions such as "what is this passage about?" or "what type of word would go there?" help students make good predictions about the approximate meaning of words. Depending on the word and/or the function of the word, often times, an approximate meaning is enough to comprehend the text.

Another question to ask when using context and structural analysis is "How important is this word to the passage?" Consider the following sentence: "Her mauve skirt fluttered as she fell over the precipice." If a student does not know *mauve* and *precipice,* he or she should ask, "Which one is more important? As a proficient reader, you would probably think that *mauve* is most likely a color, but *precipice* tells you what happened to her. Strong readers make good decisions about when to stop and figure out a word and when to simply guess at it and move on.

Getting Started

Contextual Redefinition is a good strategy for introducing the key vocabulary in a social studies selection. It helps students learn and engage deeply with the important concepts of the reading selection, and helps them practice the behaviors and thinking that proficient readers use to figure out unknown words.

Step 1: Identify Unfamiliar Words. Before students begin reading, select the word or words that will be unfamiliar to them. The words that work best are the words that contain meaningful morphemes for analysis. Prefixes such as *auto* or *tri* and root words such as *bio* or *graph* and so forth are familiar enough to students for them to make associations to new words. Having students guess the meanings of particular morphemes is far better than just telling them the meanings. By guessing, students must become actively involved in the reading.

Step 2: Guess Word Meanings. Present the word in isolation and ask students to make guesses about the meaning of the word. The only clues they have available to them at this point are their associations with the prefixes, root words, and suffixes. Remember that some of these guesses will be wrong or even funny. But it is the process of using structural analysis that is important, not proving someone's guess right or wrong.

Step 3: Refine Guesses. Present increasingly rich context clues and have students refine their guesses about what the word means as each sentence is presented. These clues can be presented through sentences with increasingly rich context, or you can use the passage from the book in which the word is used, or both.

Step 4: Verify Meanings. Direct students to look the word up in a dictionary or glossary to verify the meaning of the word. A dictionary is not always helpful if students do not have any idea what a word means. Therefore, a dictionary or glossary should be the last place they go, not the first. The purpose of these references is to verify an already good guess about the word meaning.

The Strategy in Action

The following steps show you how to implement the strategy. This activity is centered around the topic of the water supply. In this passage four terms are used that may cause difficulty for students when they read.

Water

Dry regions are found in many parts of the world, including the western United States. There are also **semiarid** regions—regions that receive a small amount of rain. Semiarid places are usually too dry for farming. However, these areas may be suitable for grazing animals.

Many areas of high mountains receive heavy snowfall in the winter. When that snow melts, it forms rivers that flow from the mountains to neighboring regions. People in dry regions use various means to bring the water where it is needed for agricultural and other uses. They build canals, reservoirs, and **aqueducts**—artificial channels for carrying water.

Some places have water deep underground in **aquifers.** These are water-bearing layers of rock, sand, or gravel. Some are quite large. For example, the Ogallala Aquifer stretches across the Great Plains from Texas to South Dakota. People drill wells to reach the water in the aquifer.

People in dry coastal areas have access to plenty of salt water. However, they typically do not have enough freshwater. In Southwest Asia this situation is common. To create a supply of freshwater, people in these places have built machines that take the salt out of seawater. This process, known as **desalinization,** is expensive and takes a lot of energy. However, in some places it is necessary.

Step 1: **Identify Unfamiliar Words.** The words *semiarid, aqueduct, aquifers,* and *desalinization* may be unfamiliar to students and are important to the understanding of the text selection.

Step 2: **Guess Word Meanings.** Students can now begin to make guesses about the meaning of the words. Here are some examples of associations that students might make with these words.

semiarid:

> *a semi is a kind of truck, semicircle is a half of a circle, semiconscious is a person who is only partly conscious, semifinal in sports is the one right before the final one.*
> *arid is a kind of deodorant*
> > *so, maybe it is half of a deodorant*

aqueduct:

> *reminds me of the bluish color, an aquarium holds fish, has something to do with water*
> *a tear duct is where the tears come out, duct tape is that silver stuff,*

when someone does duct work, they work on the pipes that vent your home

> *so, maybe it is a pipe that holds water*

aquifer:

this one is like aqueduct, probably has something to do with water too

> *something to do with water*

desalinization:

dehumidify *means "to take away the humidity,"* degrade *means "to move something down a notch" or "talk badly about something or someone"*

a saline solution is one with salt in it

> *so, probably means to take down the salt in food or something*

Step 3: Refine Guesses. Now present increasingly rich context clues and have students refine their guesses. In this case, these words are defined well in the text. But often more than one sentence is necessary to understand the concept.

Semiarid:

1. I live in a *semiarid* region of the country.
2. People that live in *semiarid* parts of the country depend on water that is either stored in dams or brought to them from somewhere else.
3. Dry regions are found in many parts of the world, including the western United States. There are also *semiarid* regions— regions that receive a small amount of rain.

Aqueduct:

1. The Romans built great *aqueducts.*
2. *Aqueducts* can help people who live in semiarid regions of the country.
3. People in dry regions use various means to bring the water where it is needed for agricultural and other uses. They build canals, reservoirs, and *aqueducts*—artificial channels for carrying water.

Aquifers:

1. *Aquifers* usually run underground.
2. People drill wells to tap into *aquifers.*
3. Some places have water deep underground in *aquifers.* These are water-bearing layers of rock, sand, or gravel.

Desalinization:

1. *Desalinization* is expensive.
2. Some people are so desperate for water, they build machines to *desalinize* seawater.
3. To create a supply of freshwater, people in these places have built machines that take the salt out of seawater. This process, known as *desalinization,* is expensive and takes a lot of energy.

Step 4: **Verify Meanings.** After students have a pretty good idea of the meaning of the words, they can clarify and refine their meanings by going to a dictionary or glossary. The glossary definitions of these four words are given below.

Semiarid: relatively dry with small amounts of rain

Aqueduct: artificial channels for carrying water

Aquifer: underground water-bearing layers of rock, sand, or gravel

Desalinization: the process in which the salt is taken out of seawater

Using the Strategy in Your Classroom

While reading, most people use a variety of strategies simultaneously to comprehend text. Structural and contextual analysis are two of the most helpful. Another one is to examine the syntax of the sentence or the way that the word functions in the sentence. The first sentences presented for *semiarid* and *aqueduct* tell students that *semiarid* is an adjective and that *aqueduct* is a noun. While presenting the sentences with increasingly rich context, make sure to help students see how each sentence gives them the very important clue of syntax.

When using structural analysis to help students associate new words with known words, you should point out that these conventions do not always apply. For example, *-er* at the end of a word means "someone who does something," so a painter is one who paints. But is a mother one who moths? Is a father one who faths? Associating familiar prefixes, root words, and suffixes usually helps students figure out the meanings of unknown words, but not always.

The powerful component of the Contextual Redefinition is the teacher modeling that occurs when teachers talk to students about what to do when they are stuck on an unknown word. Particularly struggling readers need to experience successful models of reading behavior and thinking.

Extending the Strategy

Wordbusting, also known as CSSD, is a parallel strategy to Contextual Redefinition and may help students know which strategies to use first when reading silently. The steps to Wordbusting are as follows:

1. *Context.* Use clues from the words and sentences around the word.

2. *Structure.* Look for familiar roots, prefixes, or suffixes.

3. *Sound.* Say the word aloud. It may sound like a word you know.

4. *Dictionary.* Look up the word.

Some Final Thoughts

Educators are desperate to teach students words because these words can be used during writing and speaking and to assist in thinking more clearly. Vocabulary is also a common component of standardized tests and achievement tests such as the SAT. Well-meaning teachers often assign students to copy definitions and use these words in sentences. Lists and lists of words are assigned each week in every content area. Generally, these words are presented in relative isolation from any meaningful content, only slightly learned, and rapidly forgotten.

A strategy such as Contextual Redefinition enables students to figure out the meanings of unknown words during reading on their own. In my opinion, there is more value to teaching students effective ways of figuring out unknown words independently than attempting to teach them a whole host of words. In addition to helping them learn strategies, they need to read text, both narrative and expository, in which they encounter words they do not know.

Practice the Strategy

Use these online materials to guide your students as they practice the Developing Vocabulary Knowledge strategy.

Read More about It

Cunningham, J. W., Cunningham, P. M., and Arthur, S. V. 1981. *Middle and secondary school reading.* New York: Longman.

Gifford, A. P. 2000. Broadening concepts through vocabulary development. *Reading Improvement* 37 (1): 2 –12.

Ittzes, K. 1991. Lexical guessing in isolation and context. *Journal of Reading* 34 (5): 360–66.

Simpson, P. L. 1996. Three step reading vocabulary strategy for today's content area reading classroom. *Reading Improvement* 33 (2): 76–80.

Watts, S. and Truscott, D. M. 1996. Using contextual analysis to help students become independent word learners. *The NERA Journal* 32 (3): 13–20.

Strategy 11
Taking Effective Notes

Identifying the most important ideas in a text and capturing them in the form of notes for study or writing a report can be a formidable task for many students. Any of the prereading strategies suggested in this book can help students focus on the most important points before they read. The INSERT Method (Interactive Notation System for Effective Reading and Thinking) was developed by Vaughn and Estes (1986) to assist students in clarifying their own understanding of the text and making decisions while they read. This strategy can be used to provide the assistance some students need to concentrate on important information and the structure to organize those ideas after reading.

How Can the Strategy Help My Students?

Most students, especially those who struggle with reading assignments, do not understand that comprehending text involves *responding* to it in some way. In fact, some struggling readers do not realize that *thinking* is necessary while reading. Strong readers integrate the information in the text with what they already know. They constantly make decisions or have a running conversation with themselves such as the following:

> *This point is important, but this one is a detail.*
>
> *This seems like an example used to help me understand the text.*
>
> *I already knew that.*
>
> *I didn't know that.*
>
> *This is in boldfaced type—must be a major concept.*

I don't understand this explanation.

This map must be here for a reason—probably to illustrate the important ideas.

The INSERT Method is designed to prompt students to have these types of conversations while they read. It also provides a structure for students to organize effective notes after they read.

Getting Started

Vaughn and Estes suggested that the INSERT Method could help students think more and better while they read. I adapted this method into the steps below to extend this strategy and help students capture the most important ideas into effective notes.

Step 1: **Introduce Students to Symbols in INSERT.** An endless set of symbols can be used to help students focus on the text. Which ones you choose depends on the purpose for reading and type of text. Some examples are listed below.

√	Knew this already
***	Important information
++	Supporting detail
Ex	Example of important concept
??	Don't understand this

Step 2: **Read the Text and Respond Using Symbols.** Students are not normally allowed to write in textbooks. But the INSERT Method requires that students respond in writing to the ideas in the text. Some teachers fold a sheet of paper lengthwise into three sections, place the INSERT symbols at the top with a line to indicate the page number, and instruct students to place this sheet alongside the book for notetaking. Other teachers have used blank transparency sheets for students to record their responses with a felt-tip marker. Still other teachers prefer to use "sticky" notes with the symbols printed on them or indicated

with different colors to mark passages in the text. The "sign here" pointed sticky notes seem to work best.

Step 3: Use Symbols to Organize Notes from the Reading. This is a good time to have students compare notes. That is, they can meet in small groups to share what they thought were the most important points, the details, and/or the examples presented in the text. The discussion helps students understand how to find the main idea in passages and organize information. They can then organize these main ideas in the form of notes.

The Strategy in Action

The following steps show you how to implement the strategy. This activity is centered around the topic of steam power. When you have students read a passage such as "The Age of Steam," you probably want them to appreciate how technological advances have changed the everyday lives of Americans. Steam power liberated people from power provided by human and animal labor.

The Age of Steam

Before the Industrial Revolution, people relied on natural sources of energy to do work. They used muscle power from animals or humans, waterpower from rivers, and wind power. These were the only options available.

With the development of steam power, a new source of energy became available. The first steam engines were built in the early 1700s in Europe. Engineers such as Scotsman James Watt greatly improved these early designs, making them more practical. The early steam engines were large and heavy with three main parts: the boiler, the cylinder, and the condenser. In the boiler, a fuel such as wood or coal was burned to heat water and produce steam. The steam then entered the cylinder, where it built up enough pressure to push a piston up and down. The condenser increased the engine's power by pulling steam out of the cylinder, thus speeding up the piston.

Other machinery converted the piston's motion into energy that could turn the paddlewheel of a steamboat, the wheels of a train, or the belts on a machine. These early "low-pressure" steam engines produced steady, reliable power.

Later, American Oliver Evans helped develop a more powerful steam engine. Lacking a condenser, it used steam at much higher pressure. Although it burned more fuel, Evans's simple high-pressure steam engine was ideal for steam-boats running on the Mississippi River or locomotives racing across the American countryside.

Steam power was often dangerous. As engineers on steamboats or steam trains tried to get the most power out of their engines, the high-pressure boilers often exploded, injuring or killing people. Despite the risks, engineers continued to use and improve steam engines throughout the 1800s. Gradually, factories began to use steam power, allowing them to operate in areas without access to waterpower.

Step 1: **Introduce Students to Symbols in INSERT.** Given that the major learning objective is to see that steam power moved Americans from relying on natural sources of energy to relying on ones that could be created and reproduced, you might wish to use the following symbols:

MI	Main idea
H	Historical point
E	Explanation

Step 2: **Read the Text and Respond Using Symbols.** This text has two main ideas: (1) new source of energy and (2) factories using steam power, two historical points: (1) James Watt and (2) Oliver Evans, and two explanations of how steam works: (1) three main parts and (2) applied paddlewheel. Thus, these components might be labeled as MI1, MI2, H1, H2, E1, and E2, respectively.

Step 3: **Use Symbols to Organize Notes from the Reading.** Depending on the purpose for reading, the notes could be arranged in different ways. The information could be placed into a concept map or used as part of a larger essay on the technological advancements that moved American industry and transportation along.

Using the Strategy in Your Classroom

The purpose of the INSERT Method is to engage students in the major points of the text and to help them organize their thinking. Feel free to change the symbols depending on your purpose for having students read a selection. For example, if students are reading a position statement of some sort, you may wish to use the following symbols:

A	Agree with this statement
D	Disagree with this statement
I	Interesting statement

INSERT helps students respond to and organize the ideas in the text. Categorizing the ideas in the text engages students in thinking and making decisions about the text. In time, students will make these distinctions on their own.

Extending the Strategy

Taking notes from text is an important skill that must be used to write a report or make a presentation. The Cornell or divided-page notetaking system is a popular system used in many middle and high schools. In this system the important points are listed on the left side of the paper, and the details are listed on the right. In this example the page might look like this:

Key Points	Details
Influences of steam power	1. A new source of energy. 2. Factories use steam, which allows them to operate without waterpower.
History of steam power	1. 1700s in Europe—James Watt 2. American Oliver Evans developed a more powerful steam engine.
How steam power works	1. Boiler: Fuel is burned to heat water and produce steam. 2. Cylinder: Steam is built up to push piston up and down. 3. Condenser: Increases power by pulling steam out of cylinder and speeds up the piston.

This information can easily be translated into a concept map (see Strategy 4) or a graphic organizer (see Strategy 3) to help students see the relationship of ideas.

Some Final Thoughts

The INSERT Method is a simple yet powerful strategy for helping students respond to reading their social studies textbooks. This strategy is most effective when used with a prereading strategy that activates what students know about a topic before reading or a postreading strategy such as creating a concept map or graphic organizer. The purpose of this strategy is to assist students in thinking and responding to text.

Practice the Strategy

Use these online materials to guide your students as they practice the Taking Effective Notes strategy.

Read More about It

Czarnecki, E., Rosko, D., and Fine, E. 1998. How to call up notetaking skills. *Teaching Exceptional Children* 30 (6): 14–19.

Randall, S. N. 1996. Information charts: A strategy for organizing student research. *Journal of Adolescent and Adult Literacy* 39 (7): 536–42.

Rankin, V. 1999. The thought that counts: Six skills that help kids turn notes into knowledge. *School Library Journal* 45 (8): 24–26.

Tomlinson, L. M. 1997. A coding system for notemaking in literature: Preparation for journal writing, class participation, and essay tests. *Journal of Adolescent and Adult Literacy* 40 (6): 468–76.

Vaughn, J. L. and Estes, T. H. 1986. *Reading and reasoning beyond the primary grades.* Needham Heights, MA: Allyn and Bacon.

Weisharr, M. K. and Boyle, J. R. 1999. Notetaking strategies for students with disabilities. *The Clearing House* 72 (6): 392–95.

Reading Strategies for the Social Studies Classroom
A Quick Reference Guide

Strategy 1: Previewing Text

This strategy focuses on PIC, a way to preview text. PIC stands for identifying the *P*urpose for reading, looking for *I*mportant ideas, and *C*onnecting the reading to students' prior knowledge.

- Make sure students know what to do with the information after reading.

- Students should look through the reading, noting main headings and key vocabulary as clues to the text's main ideas.

- Students should consider what they already know about the topic and ask themselves, "What would I like to find out?"

Strategy 2: Understanding Text

This strategy helps students look for signal words that identify the structure of different types of texts.

- Students survey the text, looking for the different types of readings they will need to perform.

- Students identify the signal words in the text.

- Based on the signal words, students identify the structure of the text.

- Students predict the main idea of the passage.

- Students read the text.

- Students revisit and revise their main idea predictions.

Strategy 3: Using Graphic Organizers

This strategy helps students understand and graphically display four types of expository text: cause and effect, compare and contrast, problem and solution, and sequence or chronological order.

- Students preview the material to be read.

- Students hypothesize which graphic organizer would be best to display the information and their understanding of the material.

- Students read the text silently, taking notes.

- Students work in cooperative groups to create a graphic representation of their understanding of the text.

- Students present the finished product to others in the class.

Strategy 4: Constructing Concept Maps

This strategy helps students organize main ideas and supporting details in a visual format.

- Students preview the passage.

- Students look at the headings and boldfaced terms and use this information to sketch a concept map that might display the information.

- Students read the text.

- Students use boxes, bubbles, circles, lines, arrows, and any other shapes they like to construct the concept map.

Strategy 5: Visualizing Information

This strategy shows students how to use the visual information that often accompanies text to aid their comprehension.

- Students preview the text, noting the visual information presented.

- Students ask themselves how the visual information relates to the text or why the author(s) included this information.

- Students next generate questions based on the visual aid.

- Students read the text.

- After reading, students review the visual aids to evaluate how well they represented the information in the text.

Strategy 6: Building Background Information

This strategy focuses on the Predicting and Confirming Activity, which allows students to analyze the background information they have by making predictions about the reading.

- First, provide students with some general information about the topic and pose a general question.

- Students write predictions about the text based on the initial information.

- Provide students with some new information.

- Review student predictions and turn them into questions.

- Students read the text.

- Students look back at their predictions and answer the questions generated earlier.

Strategy 7: Making Predictions

This strategy uses the List-Group-Label-Map activity to help students activate their prior knowledge by making predictions.

- Students list as many words about the topic as they can.

- Students group the words into categories based on associations.

- Students label the word groups.

- Students use these categories to make a concept map about the topic.

- Students read the text.

- After reading, students revisit the concept map, adding information they gathered while reading.

Strategy 8: Activating and Using Prior Knowledge

This strategy uses the KWL (What I *Know*, What I *Want* to Know, What I *Learned*) activity to help students activate their prior knowledge.

- Students fill out the first two columns (*Know* and *Want* to Know) of the KWL chart.

- Students next read, view, or listen to content about the topic.

- Students construct a concept map, like the ones described in Strategy 4.

- Students write a summary based on their concept maps.

Strategy 9: Anticipating Information

This strategy helps students clarify their ideas and opinions about a topic by using Anticipation Guides.

- Write four to six general statements that reflect key concepts in the content.

- Students point out statements with which they agree or disagree.

- Next, engage students in a prereading discussion. You might count and tally the *agrees* and *disagrees* for each statement.

- Students read the text.

- Students should revisit their earlier responses to the statements and see if they have changed their opinions.

- Engage students in a postreading discussion to get them to compare their responses before and after reading the text.

Strategy 10: Developing Vocabulary Knowledge

This strategy helps students figure out what to do when they encounter unfamiliar vocabulary.

- Before students begin reading, select the words that will most likely give them difficulty.

- Have students look at word parts and try to guess the word meanings.

- Present new content and have students refine their guesses.

- Have students look up the words in a dictionary or glossary to verify the meanings.

Strategy 11: Taking Effective Notes

This strategy teaches students how to use the INSERT (Interactive Notation System for Effective Reading and Thinking) Method to take notes while they are reading.

- First, you need to introduce students to the symbols of INSERT.

- Students next read the text and respond using symbols.

- Students should then use symbols to organize their notes from the reading.